HIMALAYAS

ARCTIC
-15
06 UN 2007

DORVAL
287

MADAGASCAR
15. NOV.

SAHARA
10
Arrival
02. 29. 1984

an encyclopedia
of ecology

GREAT BARRIER REEF
(10293)

DATE   07, 28 1975

CHINA
18, 1987

LAS VEGAS

19/08

LONDON, NEW YORK,
MELBOURNE, MUNICH, and DELHI

Senior Art Editor Tory Gordon-Harris
Senior Editors Elinor Greenwood and Elizabeth Haldane

Editors Lorrie Mack, Zahavit Shalev, Penny Smith, Fleur Star
Designers Clare Harris, Karen Hood, Poppy Joslin,
Laura Roberts-Jensen, Clare Shedden

Writers
Introduction and Temperate forests: Dr. Lynn Dicks
Polar regions: Chris Woodford
Tropical forests and Mountains: Michael Scott
Deserts and Grasslands: Dr. Kim Dennis-Bryan
Freshwater and Oceans: Dr. Frances Dipper

Science consultant Dr. Lynn Dicks

Publishing Manager Susan Leonard
Category Publisher Mary Ling
Picture Researcher Liz Moore
Production Controller Claire Pearson
Production Editor Siu Chan
Jacket Designers Sophia Tampakopoulos and Natalie Godwin

First published in the United States in 2008 by
DK Publishing
375 Hudson Street, New York, New York 10014

earth
matters

A ca...
availab...
ISBN 97...
Color repr...
Printed and...

FSC
© Mixe...
Product gr...
www.fsc.org
forests an...
© 1996 Forests...

Discover more at
www.dk.com

earth
matters

contents

DAVID DE ROTHSCHILD

Protecting our planet has never been more important or urgent. On my adventures to the poles of the Earth—extreme, spectacular, and dangerous locations—I have seen for myself the shrinking glaciers, melting ice sheets, and struggling polar bears.

If you're anything like me, the scale and **complexity** of the problems we face sometimes seem overwhelming and rather frightening. With *clear evidence* now showing that it's our everyday actions driving climate change, it only requires a little more **understanding**, **commitment**, and **motivation** in order for us to create the solutions our planet craves.

Inside *Earth Matters,* you will find everything you will ever want to know about Earth's ecology. From the top of the tallest mountain to the bottom of the deepest sea, from the polar wilderness to the teeming jungle, each page is crammed with easy-to-understand facts and figures, specially commissioned maps, and outstanding photography.

King penguin

Bell heather

Our home planet is **beautiful**, miraculous, and possibly *unique*
in the universe... **Earth matters.** That's for sure.

Angel fish

The *Plastiki* Adventure My goal is to publicize the problems facing our planet using the romance of adventure and the power of the internet. My next adventure is to sail a boat made entirely out of recycled plastic bottles from the US to Australia via the Great Pacific Garbage Patch——huge, floating "clouds" of plastic trash caught in a swirling vortex of ocean currents.

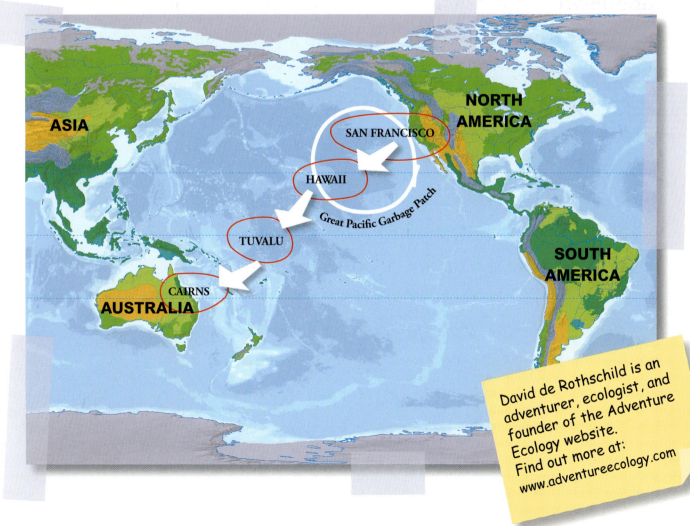

David de Rothschild is an adventurer, ecologist, and founder of the Adventure Ecology website. Find out more at: www.adventureecology.com

one person can make

"One person can make all the difference in the world. For the first time in recorded human history, we have the fate of the whole planet in our hands."

"One person can make all the difference in the world. For the first time in recorded human history, we have the fate of the whole planet in our hands."

Chrissie Hynde (b. 1951), musician

"I'd put my money on the Sun and solar energy. What a source of power! I hope we don't have to wait 'til oil and coal run out before we tackle that!"

**Thomas Edison
(1847–1931), inventor**

"We have a very small number of years left to fail or to succeed in providing a sustainable future to our species."

Jacques Cousteau (1910–1997), explorer and marine conservationist

We do not inherit the land from our ancestors, we borrow it from our children.

Native American proverb

all the difference...

"I see Earth. It is so beautiful."

Yuri Gagarin (1934–1968), cosmonaut

"The more I studied about ecology, the more I cared and wanted to do something, to help in some way even if it's a small way."

Woody Harrelson (b. 1961), actor

"YOU MUST BE THE CHANGE YOU WISH TO SEE IN THE WORLD."

Mahatma Gandhi (1869–1948), spiritual and political leader

If you want one year of prosperity, plant corn.
If you want ten years of prosperity, plant trees.
If you want one hundred years of prosperity, educate people.

Chinese proverb

"How to be green? ... It's really very simple and requires no expert knowledge or complex skills. Here's the answer. Consume less. Share more. Enjoy life."

Dr. Derek Wall, politician and professor

INTRODUCTION

Once upon a time, a long time ago (13.7 billion years ago), there was a bang and the *universe began.*

INTRODUCTION

Some call it the "Big Bang," and it seems our universe did start
with a massive, mind-bendingly huge explosion. The result was
the birth of a billion stars and from this our tiny planet emerged—

what is the **universe?**

The universe is everything that exists: all the stars, planets, rocks, dust, and gas, and all the space in between them. Each star is a sun. Many are far larger and hotter than our own Sun. Stars are grouped into galaxies—huge spirals or whirlpools full of stars. With telescopes, we can see billions of galaxies, and each one contains billions of stars. But the more we know, the more questions are thrown up, and the more mysteries emerge. We are still discovering new things about our universe all the time.

This is a spiral galaxy similar to the Milky Way called Andromeda.

When did the universe begin? Cosmologists (scientists who study the universe) believe it began over 13 billion years ago, with an enormous explosion called the "Big Bang." We can see the afterglow of that explosion in microwaves—light coming from a very long time ago—all over the universe. What happened before the Big Bang? Physics tells us there was no "before" because there was no time...

How big is the universe? All the stars you can see in the night sky are just a tiny part of the universe. If what you can see were the size of a ping pong ball, then what our telescopes can see would be the size of the entire Earth—and scientists think that our telescopes are only looking at a portion of the universe, and really it's even bigger than that! The universe is also expanding, like a balloon being inflated. Any star you look at, in any direction, is moving farther and farther away...

THE UNIVERSE

our place in space

Earth is a tiny speck of rock in the vastness of the universe. In our solar system, it is one of eight planets that circle around a star—the Sun.

Our Sun is one of several hundred billion stars grouped together in a spiral galaxy called the Milky Way. On a clear night you can see one of its arms as a streak of white across the sky. The brightest part is the center of the galaxy. The Milky Way is just one of the billions of galaxies scattered through space. All together, they form the universe.

Earth is just one of eight planets in our solar system, which lies halfway along one of the spiral arms of the Milky Way.

This is the Milky Way!

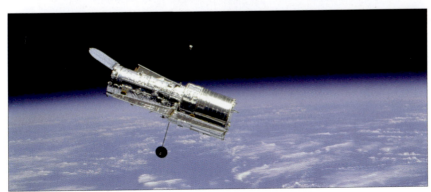

The Hubble Space Telescope was launched in 1990 and can view huge distances because it is outside the haze of the Earth's atmosphere. It can see 12 billion light-years away (one light-year is about 5.880 trillion miles, or 9.460 km), making it the most powerful telescope ever. Without it we would know far less about our universe.

just right **for life**

Earth is the only place in our solar system that sustains any known form of life—we haven't found life anywhere else in the universe. Yet our planet contains millions of different life forms, all perfectly adapted to their environments—from tiny ants to chimpanzees, jewel beetles to humankind itself, living in teeming seas, lush forests, and barren deserts. Here are the ingredients that make our Earth the perfect place to be.

1 Just the right SIZED SUN

Big stars burn out faster than small ones, and really massive stars burn out so fast that life doesn't have time to develop on any of their planets. Small stars aren't suitable either because they're prone to surface storms that can destroy life on nearby planets. Our Sun is an ideally middle-sized star that will burn for about 10 billion years.

The SUN is **865,000 million miles** (1.4 billion km) in diameter (distance across)

By comparison, Earth is so small that you can barely see it.

2 Just the right SIZED PLANET

The size of a planet controls the strength of its gravity. Jupiter is much larger than Earth, and its atmosphere is under a great deal of pressure—it would crush a spaceship like a paper cup. Mars, on the other hand, is just over half the size of Earth, and its thin atmosphere is under much, *much* less pressure. If you stood on Mars, the water in your cells would evaporate, turning to gas. Since you are 60 percent water, you would probably explode. Earth has *just* enough gravity to hold on to its atmosphere, which protects us from the Sun's harmful rays and keeps us warm (see pages 24–25).

Jupiter

 EARTH is **7,926 miles** (12,756 km) in diameter

Mars

30 million different species thrive on Earth.

Earth is called a "Goldilocks planet." This is a scientific term that refers to a planet that is neither too hot nor too cold, too big nor too small, too near its star nor too far away, to support life as we know it. It's *just right*.

Asteroid belt

Jupiter

Saturn

Uranus

Neptune

SUN

Mercury Venus Mars

EARTH

3 Just the right DISTANCE from the SUN

There is a narrow zone around each star that could support life because its temperatures allow water to be liquid. In our solar system only Earth falls within this zone. The temperature on the surface of Venus is far too hot—almost 930°F (500°C)—so water would turn into vapor. On Mars, the average temperature is a chilling -81°F (-63°C) so any water would form ice.

4 The existence of WATER

Life as we know it depends on water. There has to be just the right amount of water in liquid form, and a solid surface for it to pool on. We have some ice on Earth, and some hot springs that give off vapor, but most of our water flows freely in oceans, lakes, rivers, and streams.

5 A little help from JUPITER

Without giant planets, Earth-sized planets would suffer lots of damaging collisions from asteroids and comets. Jupiter, 11 times the size of Earth (with much stronger gravity), mops up lots of rubble in the inner solar system. The comet Shoemaker-Levy 9 was drawn in by Jupiter's gravity in 1994. The collision with the planet caused huge fireballs and scarred its surface badly. We're lucky we avoided that particular collision!

JUPITER is the biggest planet in our solar system.

life begins

The Earth finished forming more than four and a half billion years ago. For the first half a billion years, its rock was slowly cooling, forming a solid crust. Over time, **volcanoes** spat gases out from the Earth's core, forming an atmosphere of carbon dioxide, nitrogen, and water vapor. As Earth continued to cool, the water vapor turned to rain, which filled the seas. Rock fragments found in Greenland (see below) reveal that the earliest of all life forms was a type of green bacteria that started growing in these oceans three and a half billion years ago—almost as soon as the oceans were formed.

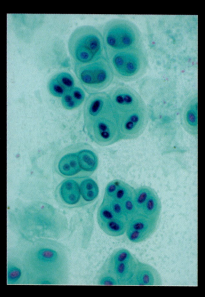

How did it start?

The oldest existing fragments of Earth's surface were found in Greenland. Dating from 3.85 billion years ago, they don't contain any fossils, but the chemicals inside them prove that life, in the form of green bacteria, already existed when the rocks were formed. Early Earth was pounded by asteroids, deadly ultraviolet radiation, and cosmic rays—there was no ozone layer to protect it then, so it was very radioactive. There are four main theories about how this harsh environment first produced life.

What is life? Living things (things that can grow and reproduce) are made of cells—each one is a fatty-membrane sac full of chemicals. For the first three billion years of Earth's existence, all living things had only one cell. In your body, there are at least 10 trillion cells.

Key to life

Cells contain strands of DNA—a genetic code that tells your body how to grow.

1. PRIMORDIAL SOUP

Life may have begun spontaneously, from reactions between the atmosphere and early oceans. Bolts of electricity from the atmosphere hitting the sloshy mixture that contained the elements of early Earth could have produced fats, proteins, and sugars—the building blocks of living cells.

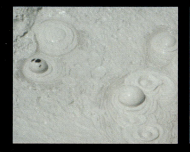

2. DEEP-SEA VENTS

Deep beneath the oceans are "hydrothermal vents," where hot volcanic gases bubble up from the Earth's core. Some bacteria, instead of needing sunlight or food, can survive here on energy from sulphur. Early life forms may have developed in this unique habitat, where they were also safe from asteroid attacks.

3. LIFE FROM SPACE

The basic chemicals of life may have come from outer space. Some meteorites contain amino acids—organic molecules that are the building blocks of living cells. Several thousand tons of these molecules land on Earth every year, and these may have resulted in the first sparks of life.

4. ONE BIG EXPERIMENT

Maybe life was sent to Earth by aliens. But could anything living survive a journey through space, with no air or water, and so cold that atoms stop vibrating? It's just possible a microorganism could make it inside a meteorite. After all, bacteria have survived for 25 million years inside the stomach of a fossilized bee.

the story of life

Primitive life arrived on Earth nearly **4 billion years** ago, but it took another *3 billion years* for animals as we know them to form from groups of cells. These time scales are almost *impossible* to imagine, so think of them as one 24-hour day.

03:25 SLIMEWORLD **2**
The chemicals of life start harvesting energy, growing, and reproducing. At first, there are only primitive green bacteria, which produce slime. Later, oxygen begins to build up in the atmosphere.

00:00 EARTH FORMS **1**
Our Earth forms at the same time as the rest of the solar system, nine billion years after the Big Bang.

Until midafternoon, bacteria are the only living things.

How does our 24-hour history of life on Earth work? Imagine the world formed at midnight and we have just reached the next midnight. On this time scale every second represents 52,662 years, and each minute represents over three million years.

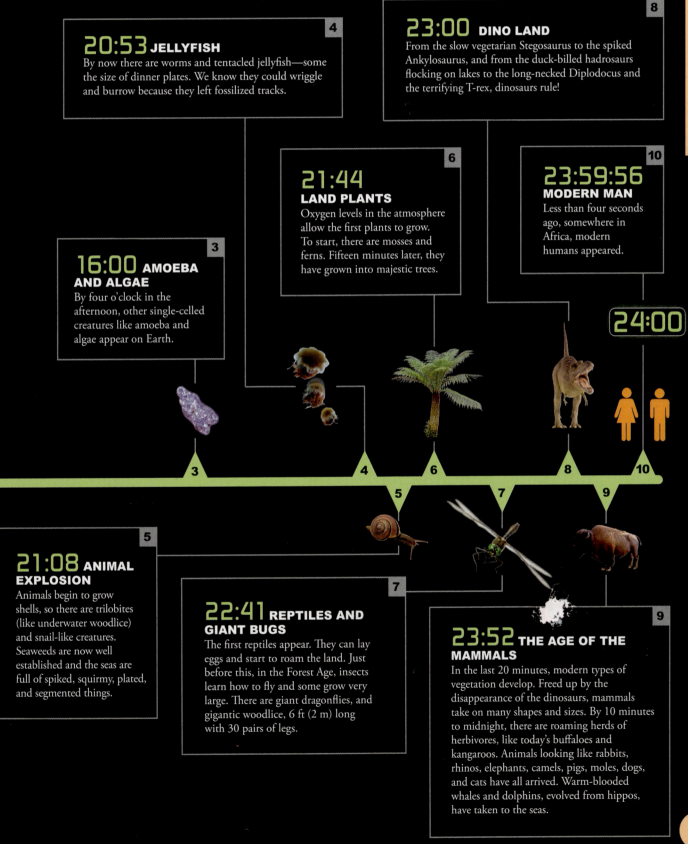

20:53 JELLYFISH

4

By now there are worms and tentacled jellyfish—some the size of dinner plates. We know they could wriggle and burrow because they left fossilized tracks.

23:00 DINO LAND

8

From the slow vegetarian Stegosaurus to the spiked Ankylosaurus, and from the duck-billed hadrosaurs flocking on lakes to the long-necked Diplodocus and the terrifying T-rex, dinosaurs rule!

21:44

6

LAND PLANTS

Oxygen levels in the atmosphere allow the first plants to grow. To start, there are mosses and ferns. Fifteen minutes later, they have grown into majestic trees.

23:59:56

10

MODERN MAN

Less than four seconds ago, somewhere in Africa, modern humans appeared.

16:00 AMOEBA

3

AND ALGAE

By four o'clock in the afternoon, other single-celled creatures like amoeba and algae appear on Earth.

24:00

21:08 ANIMAL

5

EXPLOSION

Animals begin to grow shells, so there are trilobites (like underwater woodlice) and snail-like creatures. Seaweeds are now well established and the seas are full of spiked, squirmy, plated, and segmented things.

22:41 REPTILES AND

7

GIANT BUGS

The first reptiles appear. They can lay eggs and start to roam the land. Just before this, in the Forest Age, insects learn how to fly and some grow very large. There are giant dragonflies, and gigantic woodlice, 6 ft (2 m) long with 30 pairs of legs.

23:52 THE AGE OF THE

9

MAMMALS

In the last 20 minutes, modern types of vegetation develop. Freed up by the disappearance of the dinosaurs, mammals take on many shapes and sizes. By 10 minutes to midnight, there are roaming herds of herbivores, like today's buffaloes and kangaroos. Animals looking like rabbits, rhinos, elephants, camels, pigs, moles, dogs, and cats have all arrived. Warm-blooded whales and dolphins, evolved from hippos, have taken to the seas.

a changing world

The Earth has **changed** dramatically over time. Its temperature has veered between tropical and icy. Its surface is constantly shifting, moving continents and creating mountains. And Earth's species have changed, too, none with such drastic consequences as the development of humankind.

200 million years ago

135 million years ago

10 million years ago

Jigsaw map
Because Earth's plates move constantly, the world once looked very different from the way it looks today. The west of Africa and the east of South America match, like pieces of a huge jigsaw. In the early dinosaur years they were joined, but they started to separate over 150 million years ago and they've been drifting apart ever since.

Humans arrive Humans belong to a species of ape called *Homo sapiens*. Our direct ancestors first appeared just under two million years ago. As they spread across the Earth's surface, the changes they brought were immense. They learned how to hunt and eat big mammals and they tamed wild animals. They also began to live in colonies and farm the land, thereby changing the face of the world forever.

Many species, like the woolly mammoth, became extinct after coming into contact with humans—clever pack-hunting predators with dogs and spears.

The world map—as it was

1. Man's origins are found below the Sahara Desert in Africa. During the ice ages humans were able to cross the desert and spread into soutwest Asia.

Flickering thermostat We live in somewhat chilly times, with huge ice sheets at the Poles, but Earth, during its history, has been much colder than it is now—and much hotter too. For the last 2½ million years, it's as if someone has been turning the planet's thermostat up, then down, then up again, about every 100,000 years.

SNOWBALL EARTH
Between 900 and 600 million years ago, the Earth was probably covered in ice four separate times. Because volcanoes pumped carbon dioxide into the atmosphere, things slowly warmed up.

HOT DINOS
Carbon dioxide in the atmosphere traps the Sun's heat. In dinosaur times, there was much more than there is now. The planet was so warm there was no ice at the poles.

Tectonic plates There are seven major tectonic plates and 23 smaller ones—and they are moving all the time, some more than 3 in (8 cm) a year. Earthquakes happen along fault lines where two plates are moving in opposite directions. Big valleys form where two plates are moving apart.

The crusty surface of the Earth floats on the soft mantle beneath. The closer to the center of the Earth you go, the hotter it becomes. In the center there is a core of molten iron.

when humans were advancing

2. Later, about 50,000 years ago, they spread to Europe...

3. The last place they reached was the Americas, perhaps 12,000 years ago. When humans arrived in the Americas, they found hordes of impressive large mammals. In the north, there were giant bison, mammoths, and several kinds of large camel.

The white areas indicate ice

2

3

4

' ... and into Australia.

In South America, they hunted giant ground sloths and other easy prey for meat. 75 different species were extinct within a thousand years of people arriving.

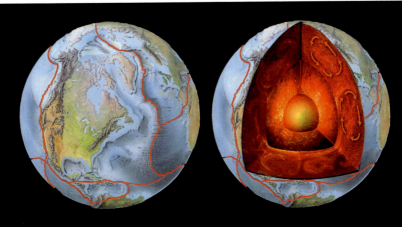

One of the oldest known cities is called Catal Huyuk, in Turkey. Farming people lived there 8,500 years ago, and they built elaborate decorated buildings.

our crowded world

Homo sapiens has been the most **successful** of species—mankind has literally **taken over** the Earth. The world population reached *6 billion* in **October 1999**. By **summer 2005**, it had reached *6.5 billion*. **In 2006,** we added more than 90 million people to the planet.

More than four babies are born every second. In the time you've spent reading this paragraph, there have been 20 new arrivals. For every four babies born, fewer than two people die, which is why the population keeps growing. If we continued at this rate, there would be 44 billion people on Earth by the end of this century. It is much more likely that the population will stabilize as people have fewer babies. The latest estimates suggest the population will peak at around 9.22 billion in 2075.

The latest estimates suggest the population

China has the most people There are over 1.3 billion Chinese people. India has over 1.1 billion and is expected to have more people than China in the next few decades. Between them, China and India have a third of all the people on Earth. The next most populous country is the US, which has around 300 million.

Where do they all live? In 2007, for the first time ever, half the people on Earth live in cities. The number of people living in urban areas will have grown from 309 million in 1950 to 3.9 billion by 2030. More people need more housing and sanitation, which produces more pollution, more concrete, and fewer green spaces.

Biodiversity is threatened All these people are having a serious impact on the rest of Earth's inhabitants. Many species are being lost forever, because we are making such great changes to the places they live. There are between 10 and 30 million species on Earth but thousands, like the tiger, are in danger.

The sixth mass extinction...

Scientists think we are losing 30,000 species a year. That's three distinct species lost forever, every hour. There have been five previous episodes of mass extinction in the history of life. Each happened because of major geological events, like the asteroid that brought the end of the dinosaurs. There is no doubt we are in the middle of the sixth mass extinction. Almost a quarter of all the world's mammal species, and one in eight bird species, are likely to be extinct in the next 25 years. But the cause is different this time. There is no major geological event—just one species on Earth damaging habitats and altering the atmosphere.

Cockroaches and rats are flourishing, however.

¼ of all mammal species— LOST?

Population in billions

7
6
5
4
3
2
1
0

1600   1700   1800   1900   2000

our atmosphere

Our atmosphere floats above our heads, like an unseen blanket around the world. Its existence is why our planet is such a lively place to be! It keeps Earth at the right temperature for plants to thrive and produce the life-giving gas—oxygen.

Energy from the Sun arrives on Earth in "short" waves called "solar radiation."

THE ATMOSPHERE HAS FOUR LAYERS

300 miles (500 km)
Satellite

Shuttle

Northern lights

50 miles (85 km)

Meteors

30 miles (50 km)

Weather balloon

ozone layer

about 6 miles (0-10 km)
Jumbo jet

Mount Everest

THERMOSPHERE

MESOSPHERE

STRATOSPHERE

TROPOSPHERE

AIR THAT WE BREATH

It's remarkable that there is so much oxygen in the Earth's atmosphere. For one thing, oxygen is unusually reactive, so it binds easily with lots of other elements to form life-giving compounds like water. Also, it's the one gas that all animal life on Earth needs to survive. So how does so much free oxygen get into the atmosphere? It's only there because plants and microbes continually create it.

78% Nitrogen

21% Oxygen

0.9% Argon

0.1% Other gases
(carbon dioxide, methane, water vapor, helium, neon, hydrogen)

Layers of air The atmosphere has four layers. The air we breathe is in the troposphere. In fact, 80–90% of Earth's air is in the troposphere, held there by gravity. Almost all the rest of the air is in the stratosphere, above the clouds, where aircraft fly. Outside a plane window, the air is too thin to breathe. Higher up, in the mesosphere, it becomes very cold, dropping to a shivery -130°F (-90°C). Then, in the thermosphere, it gets hotter and hotter the higher up you go. It can be up to 2,730°F (1,500°C) up there. There is no sharp edge to the atmosphere—it gradually thins out and becomes space.

6%

6% of solar radiation is reflected straight back to space by molecules in the atmosphere.

Without the atmosphere, Earth's average temperature would be 20°F (-6°C).

10%

10% of solar radiation bounces off the Earth's surface and back to space.

84% of solar radiation is absorbed by the rocks, soil, and water on Earth, where it changes into "long" waves—the type of heat picked up by an infrared camera. Some of these waves are stopped from dispersing into space by the atmosphere.

84%

and the greenhouse effect

The greenhouse effect Water vapor, carbon dioxide, methane, and some other gases in the atmosphere absorb long-wave heat radiation, and send it back to Earth again. It's like what happens when you wrap yourself in a duvet. The heat from your body doesn't escape, but some is absorbed by the duvet. Some of it goes back to your body, and gradually you warm up, but you don't keep getting hotter and hotter because some of the duvet's warmth escapes into the air.

94% of the Sun's heat enters through the atmosphere.

Some heat escapes out of the atmosphere. But most is reflected back by greenhouse gases.

What's gone wrong? Greenhouse gases are increasing because we have upset the balance of the atmosphere by burning fossil fuels, and through other activities that produce greenhouse gases like carbon dioxide and methane. These keep more heat inside the atmosphere, which means the Earth warms up.

the ozone layer

What does it do? Ozone is a highly reactive molecule that exists in a 4.3 miles (7 km) thick layer in the stratosphere. The ozone layer absorbs most of the harmful ultraviolet radiation from the Sun, preventing it from reaching Earth. Without it, sunlight would be very damaging to our bodies, causing sunburn, skin cancer, and eye cataracts.

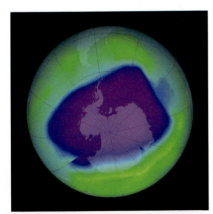

In 1985, British scientists found that almost half the ozone over Antarctica had disappeared. This shocked the world. It was because gases called chlorofluorocarbons (CFCs) had been building up in the stratosphere and these continually destroy ozone for 100 years.

CFCs were used in aerosols and to cool fridges. Now, they are hardly used at all. The rapid phase-out of CFCs shows that all the countries in the world can work together to change things quickly, if necessary.

Good news: the hole in the ozone layer is mending and will return to normal by 2050.

the carbon

A diamond crystal is 100% pure carbon.

There is a lot of talk about carbon. But what is it? And where does it come from? Carbon is a natural substance, and one of the chemical elements. In its pure form, it mostly exists as a black solid (coal) or an extremely hard transparent crystal (diamond). Carbon forms only a small part of the Earth itself—less than one percent—but it's a vital element in our bodies. All the chemicals in

A lump of coal is 95% carbon.

PENCIL "LEAD" IS NOT LEAD AT ALL. IT'S MOSTLY GRAPHITE, A SOFT FORM OF PURE CARBON.

Carbon atoms move in a natural cycle between land, water, and the atmosphere. But humans have upset the balance...

IN WATER

Carbon dioxide dissolves in water and moves from the atmosphere into the ocean. Some (usually less) also moves from the ocean to the atmosphere by a process called "diffusion."

THE ATMOSPHERE

absorption

diffusion

Like land plants, ocean plants use carbon dioxide from the water for a process called "photosynthesis" (using light to help make food). They also store carbon.

Finally, water containing carbon moves from the ocean depths to the surface. Some of the ocean's carbon then moves from the surface to the atmosphere.

diffusion

photosynthesis

respiration

When the plants and animals die, they rot in the water, dissolving or sinking to the ocean floor. There they are buried and crushed by the pressure of water above. Eventually, they turn into rocks or fossil fuels.

Ocean animals eat ocean plants and absorb the carbon they store. Both plants and animals release carbon dioxide back into the water through respiration (breathing).

Some sea creatures can take carbon out of the water and use it to make their shells. When these creatures die, their carbon-rich shells dissolve or settle on the ocean floor. Then they too get compacted and gradually turn into fossil fuel, limestone, or chalk.

decay

26

compaction

cycle

living things have an underlying structure of carbon. It also joins with oxygen to form an important gas in Earth's atmosphere—carbon dioxide. Carbon moves around on Earth more than any other element in something called the "carbon cycle."

The Earth is less than 1% carbon

... but our bodies are 18% carbon

We're made from exactly the same stuff as all other living things. Carbon chains form the basic structure of all the most complex materials inside us, including proteins, fats, and even bone.

Carbon is the basis of life on Earth.

ON LAND

All plants take carbon dioxide from the atmosphere through photosynthesis. Trees store carbon in their wood as they grow. Cutting down lots of trees all over the world slows the removal of carbon dioxide from the air.

photosynthesis

respiration

Plants also release carbon into the atmosphere through respiration.

compaction

When plants die, they rot and become part of the soil. After a long time, some of this soil gets packed down and becomes fossil fuels like coal and oil.

WHAT PEOPLE DO

Humans have a big influence on the carbon cycle. When we take fossil fuels out of the ground and burn them for energy, the carbon in them turns into carbon dioxide and enters the atmosphere. But this carbon has been out of circulation for hundreds of millions of years. Rapidly adding it to the air is upsetting the balance.

combustion

combustion

Burning trees also puts carbon dioxide into the air. This process doesn't normally upset the balance because the carbon was only just taken out of the air, by the trees themselves, as they grew.

extraction

Both the burning of fossil fuels and deforestation move carbon stored in fuel and trees to the atmosphere.

trees and plants turn into compacted soil   **FOSSIL FUELS**   **fuels are taken from the ground**

global WARMING

The carbon cycle Because people on Earth are burning so much fossil fuel and cutting down so many forests, the carbon cycle is off-balance. There is more carbon going into the atmosphere through burning than leaving it by photosynthesis.

GLOBAL WARMING FACTS AND STATS

The rise in world temperatures is called global warming. This is due in part to the amount of methane and carbon dioxide in the atmosphere (shown to the right). The increase in carbon dioxide comes from four main sectors (shown below).

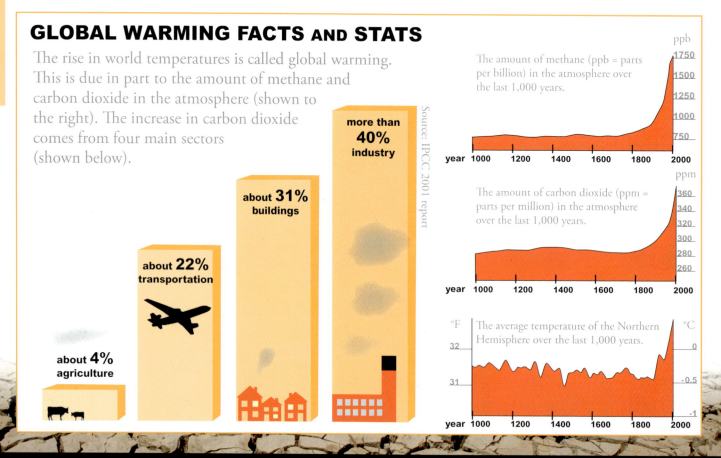

about **4%** agriculture

about **22%** transportation

about **31%** buildings

more than **40%** industry

Source: IPCC 2001 report

The amount of methane (ppb = parts per billion) in the atmosphere over the last 1,000 years.

ppb
1750
1500
1250
1000
750

year 1000 1200 1400 1600 1800 2000

The amount of carbon dioxide (ppm = parts per million) in the atmosphere over the last 1,000 years.

ppm
360
340
320
300
280
260

year 1000 1200 1400 1600 1800 2000

The average temperature of the Northern Hemisphere over the last 1,000 years.

°F   °C
32   0
31   -0.5
      -1

year 1000 1200 1400 1600 1800 2000

So far, the world has warmed

The danger from cows' bottoms

Methane is increasing, too, and it is eight times better at warming the Earth than carbon dioxide! Methane comes from rotting waste and wet paddy fields. It is also burped out—from both ends—in huge quantities by grass-eating animals such as cows. The more people there are on Earth eating meat, rice, and throwing out garbage, the more methane we produce.

MOPPING UP

Earth's seas and vegetation are absorbing some of the extra CO_2. Plants are growing more lushly. Oceans are becoming more acidic because of it. Perhaps the oceans and plants are reaching the peak of their ability to absorb extra gases.

The amount of greenhouse gases (methane and carbon dioxide) being released into the atmosphere has gone up dramatically, and so have world temperatures. This is because more greenhouse gases in the atmosphere trap more heat.

Q How do we know global warming is caused by us?

A There is plenty of uncertainty about the science of global warming: how much will it warm up? Where will there be more rain? or less? and so forth. But most of the world's scientists agree, without doubt, that **human greenhouse gas emissions** are responsible...

... whether they come from our factories, the boilers in our houses, our cars, power plants, or farms.

by 1.37°F (0.76°C) since 1900.

WARMING WORLD
Already, there is less snow and ice in the world. The great ice sheets in Antarctica (in the south) and Greenland (in the north) are melting, adding an estimated 22 billion tons (20 billion metric tons) of water each year to the sea.

NATURE'S RHYTHMS
The growing season has lengthened across much of the northern hemisphere. Japan's famous cherry blossom now blooms five days earlier on average in Tokyo than it did 50 years ago.

BIRD WATCHING
Animals and birds are entering new territories and higher altitudes because of increasing warmth. Inuits in the Canadian Arctic have spotted previously unseen birds such as robins. But, like many animals in this book, not all fauna can keep up with the changes.

in the top 12 warmest years ever recorded.

the search for energy

Energy flows so easily into our daily lives, we hardly notice it. Every time you drive in a car, take a hot shower, switch on a light, or watch TV, you use power that has traveled around the world. What's more, everything you use, including what you eat and the clothes you wear, has taken lots of energy to grow or to make, and find its way to you.

FOSSIL FUELS Once the remains of living things, fossil fuels such as coal, oil, and natural gas come from underground. They are fairly cheap, so people use their energy to do things they could do just as well by themselves, like traveling short distances in a car. But fossil fuels won't last forever, and burning them is harming our atmosphere—they are responsible for over 80 percent of carbon dioxide emissions caused by humans. If we carry on burning them until they run out, the world's temperature could rise by more than 7.2°F (4°C). We urgently need to reduce energy use, and find new sources.

Where does OUR

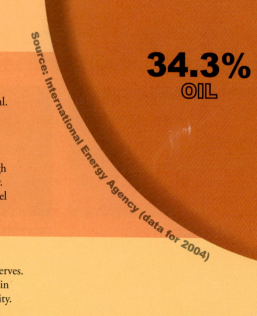

25.1%
COAL

34.3%
OIL

Source: International Energy Agency (data for 2004)

COAL
Coal is burned to create heat or, in power plants, to drive steam turbines that generate electricity.

HOW MUCH IS LEFT? There is enough coal in the ground to power the world for more than 1,000 years. Even now, developing industrial countries like China and India are busy building new coal-fired power plants.

OIL
Large reserves of oil were first discovered in the early 20th century. Because it's a liquid, oil is easier to work with than coal. It can be refined into fuels like gasoline and diesel to run cars, trucks, airplanes, and heating systems. It's also used to make products like plastics, medicines, and detergents.

HOW MUCH IS LEFT? Some experts think there is still enough oil underground to power the world for the rest of this century. Others believe that world oil production is close to its peak level now, and will soon decrease.

NATURAL GAS
Natural gas is actually methane that has collected above oil reserves. It's the last fossil fuel to be exploited and was first used widely in the 1930s and 1940s. Like coal, it's burned for heat or electricity.

HOW MUCH IS LEFT? Experts believe there is enough natural gas to last out the century, but beyond that, it's likely to become very expensive and difficult to extract.

Until about 150 years ago, humans burned wood for heating and cooking, and used animals for moving things around. But since fossil fuels became widely available, world energy use has shot up, and demand is still rising fast.

NUCLEAR ENERGY Nuclear reactors generate electricity using energy from inside atoms. Here, uranium atoms are split apart, releasing masses of energy. The first nuclear power plant opened in the United States of America in 1960, and there are now 435 similar plants around the world—104 of them in the US. Some countries rely more on nuclear power than others—it provides half of Sweden's electricity, and a huge 78 percent of France's electricity.

RENEWABLE ENERGY Unlike fossil fuels, renewable energy sources will never be used up—the energy just keeps on coming. Among the natural sources that can generate electricity or make fuels are sunlight (collected in solar panels), wind (powering tall turbines, below), water (harnessed to make hydroelectricity from waterfalls and dams), ocean waves, Earth's heat trapped under the ground, and growing plants.

energy come from?

20.9%
NATURAL GAS

6.5%
NUCLEAR

13.2%
RENEWABLES

Renewable energy breakdown
- 10.6% burning biomass or waste
- 2.2% hydroelectric (water) power
- 0.4% all other renewables

SAVING ENERGY Because fossil fuels are cheap, our buildings, our transportation, and even our power generators waste a great deal of it. For each unit of electrical power that arrives at your house, two units have been lost along the way, mostly in the form of heat. Experts have worked out that, by 2020, we could cut world greenhouse gas emissions in half—just by saving energy and doing things more efficiently.

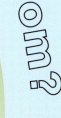

Energy-saving lightbulb

water of life

People need water for drinking, growing food, and keeping clean, and we also require large amounts for industry. The amount of water being used is increasing all the time——while Earth's population tripled in the 20th century, its water use increased six-fold. As standards of living rise, people want cleaner surroundings, and they eat a wider variety of food (leading to increasingly intensive farming). These conditions require even more water. We are already taking half the water in rivers, lakes, and streams for our own use, but wild animals and plants need it, too.

ONLY 1% OF THE WORLD'S WATER IS DRINKABLE

At least two-thirds of the water humans use is for farming.

Most of this water is for irrigation—watering plants. Many crops are sprayed with huge sprinklers, but this method wastes a lot of water through evaporation on hot days. Other systems use leaky pipes running between the plants at soil level.

TO HAVE...

In rich countries, most people have an unlimited supply of fresh clean water that flows out of faucets in their kitchen and bathroom.

... AND HAVE NOT

But in many countries, people have little access to clean water. Some women in rural Africa spend a quarter of their time carrying water.

WATER FACTS AND STATS

ONLY THREE PERCENT OF THE WORLD'S WATER IS FRESHWATER. OF THIS...

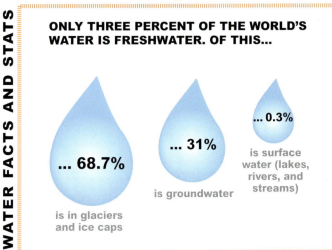

... 68.7%
is in glaciers and ice caps

... 31%
is groundwater

... 0.3%
is surface water (lakes, rivers, and streams)

THE WATER CYCLE

Water evaporates from the surface of the sea and enters the atmosphere as a gas. Some of it condenses into tiny droplets that we see as clouds. These then fall as rain or snow. Some rainwater is taken up by plants, some runs into long-term storage underground (becoming "groundwater"), and some flows into rivers and streams. This last source is where humans get most of their water.

water droplets form clouds

precipitation (rain or snow)

SUN

water evaporates from plants, lakes, and rivers

water evaporates from the ground

water evaporates from the sea

GROUNDWATER

SEA

water returns to the sea in rivers and streams

Groundwater can be thousands of years old—some of the water under London, England, for example, has been there for about 20,000 years.

Different crops need different amounts of water. Rice and cotton use quite a lot, but coffee is the thirstiest crop of all.

People use much more water than you might think.

AMOUNT OF WATER USED TO PRODUCE:

2.5 gallons (10 liters) per flush

3 gallons (13 liters)

18 gallons (70 liters)

630 gallons (2,400 liters)

700 gallons (2,700 liters)

100,000 gallons (400,000 liters)

AVERAGE WATER CONSUMPTION PER PERSON PER DAY (IN LITERS)

8,000
7,000
6,000
5,000
4,000
3,000
2,000
1,000
0

US   Britain   Botswana

HOW ONE PERSON USES WATER (AVERAGES ONLY)

■ 0.2% for drinking

■ 4.2% for washing, cooking, cleaning, flushing

■ 30.6% in manufactured goods (car, bike, TV, etc.)

■ 65% in food

high-waste society

Hundreds of thousands of tons of plastic, glass, metal, and even electronics, are thrown away every day. A hundred years ago, this kind of waste *hardly existed*. People reused things at home. They burned or

In rich countries each person produces *five to ten times* their own BODY WEIGHT in garbage each year.

So what happens to all the garbage?

It's recycled

60% of what you throw away can be recycled or composted. Glass, paper, cardboard, metals, and plastics can be crushed, pulped, or melted, and used again. This fleece, for example, is made from recycled bottles.

So what about industrial waste?

Only 10 percent of waste is household. Factories also produce waste, but because this often consists of one material (like broken-up concrete or ash) another use can sometimes be found for it.

As landfill sites fill up fast, we need to rethink our approach to garbage.
Reduce—buy less stuff.
Reuse—think of other uses for things before throwing them out.
Recycle—separate out garbage to things that can be recycled, and things that can't.
See this website for lots of handy tips: www.epa.gov

composted waste paper, food, and grass clippings. They didn't buy large quantities of packaged goods. We need to go back to how we used to be and **reduce, reuse,** and **recycle**.

HOUSEHOLD WASTE

NATURAL WASTE

MANUFACTURED PRODUCTS

About two-thirds of household waste comes from manufactured products, the rest from our food or garden.

It's composted

Composting is nature's way of dealing with waste. Food and grass clippings (or "green waste") are easily broken down by bacteria and other microbes. Paper and cardboard (or brown waste") can be composted too. Left in a pile in the corner of the yard, green waste will slowly change into dark compost that can improve the soil. Add worms to the mix and fertilizer is made even more quickly.

It's burned

Household waste can be burned, or heated in a big furnace without air in a process called "pyrolysis." This gets rid of much of the waste, and the heat can be used to generate electricity by heating water to drive a steam turbine.

The difficult wastes

The toughest wastes to deal with are hazardous wastes, such as batteries and computer parts, that contain toxic substances. These should be disposed of carefully, but in reality, they often end up in ordinary landfill sites.

It's dumped in landfill

Landfill sites are often old holes in the ground where rock has been quarried. The garbage going into them has lots of food, paper, and yard waste, which rots and creates methane, a greenhouse gas. What remains after the rotting is a foul liquid that can seep into groundwater, carrying with it toxic chemicals from hazardous wastes. Space in landfills is running out fast.

EXPORTING WASTE

Many rich countries export hundreds of thousands of tons of waste a year to countries where it can be handled more cheaply. Much of it ends up in China, which buys large quantities of waste plastic, paper, and cardboard, as well as electronic waste. The huge freight ships that carry manufactured goods from China to Europe and the US often return to China filled with lightweight waste.

sustainable life

Planet Earth provides all the resources we need to live—air to breathe, water to drink, soil to grow crops in, fuels to burn, and materials, like metals, to build things. Most of the Earth's resources are constantly being made on Earth. Some are made quickly like wood when trees grow, or freshwater when rain falls. Some take thousands of years to form, like soil. And some are limited, like land.

Land use Land is a very basic resource, because it is needed to grow plants, which are used for food, fuel, and materials. The world's land is not divided fairly at the moment—people in industrialized countries use far more than their fair share to support their lifestyle. If people in developing countries like India and China start consuming as much fuel and food, the world will not be able to support us all.

5.4 HECTARES EACH

= 3 planet earths

If the 5 billion people in the developing world used as much land as the 1.5 billion in the industrial world (5.4 hectares, or 13.3 acres, on average per person) we would need three Earths to live on.

What is your eco footprint?

Your footprints on Earth One way of seeing how sustainable your activities are is to measure your ecological footprint. This is not a foot-shaped mark in the ground! It is a number that tells you how much of the Earth's resources you use. An ecological footprint is the amount of land that would be needed to grow all the food, fuel, and materials you use. It is measured in hectares. (One hectare equals 2½ acres or 0.01 sq km.)

Already, the average ecological footprint for the whole world is 2.2 hectares, higher than the sustainable level of 1.8 hectares each.

US
9.7 hectares of land needed for each person

UK
5.6

World average
2.2

Brazil
2.1

Sustainable average
1.8

China
1.6

India
0.7

1.8 hectares per person is a sustainable footprint for today's population.

SUSTAINABLE VS UNSUSTAINABLE

Going on forever The word "sustain" means to keep going——if something is "sustainable," it can continue forever. We can only sustain the Earth's resources by consuming them at the same rate——or more slowly——than they are being produced.

SEAWEED Seaweed is harvested in many countries. Farmers have long used it as a fertilizer. Now it's also used as a food supplement, and chemicals from it are used to thicken cosmetics and food. In France, the harvest is strictly managed by law. Removing the "holdfasts," where the seaweeds attach to the rock, is prohibited. And each area that is cut must be left to regrow.

FISHING The worst case of humans overusing a natural resource at the moment is sea fishing. So many fish are being caught that wild fish populations have collapsed in many places. The fish cannot reproduce fast enough to replace the fish that are eaten. Fish species many of us eat regularly, like cod and tuna, may never recover.

ORGANIC FARMERS Organic farmers are very careful to protect their soil, so that over time it builds up and improves, rather than being blown or washed away. Unlike ordinary farmers, they seldom leave bare soil exposed over winter. They leave crop stubbles or plant a cover crop to protect the soil. They also add compost to the soil and plant hedges as windbreaks.

PALM HARVEST Some resources are overharvested for surprising purposes. American and Canadian churches import 30 million palm fronds for Palm Sunday. They come from Mexico and Guatemala, and rain-forest conservation groups say many are taken from wild rain forests. More palm plants are taken than the forest can regrow.

What is your carbon footprint?

Carbon footprint Your carbon footprint is the number of tons of carbon (in the form of carbon dioxide) released into the Earth's atmosphere per year as a result of your daily life. Carbon footprints measure your contribution to climate change. To be completely sustainable, each person should have a carbon footprint of close to zero. In theory, this is possible because carbon you emit can be "offset" (recovered) by things that remove carbon from the atmosphere, like planting a tree. In practice, the figures are very complex.

Australia
17.29
average carbon footprint

Australians have the highest average carbon footprint, followed by Americans. People in these countries have an energy-expensive lifestyle. They have lots of possessions, drive long distances, and use a lot of energy-hungry appliances like air-conditioners.

Germany
10.46

Sweden
5.91

World average
4.44

Mexico
3.84

Egypt
1.97

Cambodia
0.05

To be completely sustainable, each person should have a carbon footprint of ZERO.

ecosystems and

The biosphere includes all the water on the Earth's surface, the soils, the rocks, and much of the air. It extends to the bottom of the sea, and reaches as high in the sky as birds fly. The deepest place life has been found is the Mariana Trench, in the Pacific Ocean near the Phillippines, where bacteria live in the mud 7 miles (11 km) under

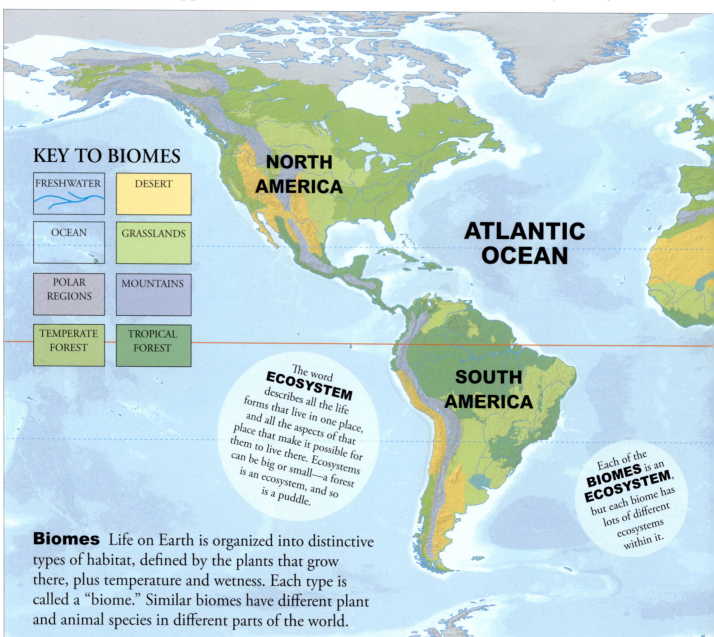

KEY TO BIOMES

FRESHWATER

OCEAN

POLAR REGIONS

TEMPERATE FOREST

DESERT

GRASSLANDS

MOUNTAINS

TROPICAL FOREST

NORTH AMERICA

ATLANTIC OCEAN

SOUTH AMERICA

The word **ECOSYSTEM** describes all the life forms that live in one place, and all the aspects of that place that make it possible for them to live there. Ecosystems can be big or small—a forest is an ecosystem, and so is a puddle.

Each of the **BIOMES** is an **ECOSYSTEM**, but each biome has lots of different ecosystems within it.

Biomes Life on Earth is organized into distinctive types of habitat, defined by the plants that grow there, plus temperature and wetness. Each type is called a "biome." Similar biomes have different plant and animal species in different parts of the world.

POLAR REGIONS
The land near the poles is covered by ice all year. Bordering this is the tundra, where it is still too cold for trees to grow—only grasses, mosses, and lichens survive.

TEMPERATE FOREST
Forests thrive in middle latitudes, which have winters and summers. Where it's very dry or very cold for some of the year, the trees are evergreen, with waxy needles.

DESERTS
In between the tropical and the temperate regions are hot, cloudless, very dry regions called deserts. Here, plant life is sparse and there is lots of sand.

GRASSLANDS
Between forests and deserts lie vast areas of grassy ground. In North America, these are called prairies, in Africa, savannas, in South America, pampas, and in Europe, steppes.

biomes

From 1991 until 1993, eight people lived inside a sealed, artificial biosphere—an enormous greenhouse—in Arizona. The idea was to see if humans could live like this on another planet. It didn't work. After a year and a half, oxygen had to be added because the inhabitants couldn't breathe, and many of the animals had died.

the sea. The highest recorded animal is a Ruppell's vulture, which crashed into an aircraft flying 37,000 ft (11,300 m) above West Africa in 1973.

EUROPE

ASIA

AFRICA

EQUATOR

INDIAN OCEAN

PACIFIC OCEAN

AUSTRALIA

Of course, not all of England is **TEMPERATE FOREST**, or all of India **TROPICAL FOREST**, but the land in these countries would revert to their given biomes if they were left untouched.

The **EDEN PROJECT** in Cornwall, UK, has two greenhouses with artificial biomes—one tropical forest, and one temperate forest.

SOUTHERN OCEAN

TROPICAL FORESTS

Tropical rain forests are extremely hot and wet, so the trees are green all year round. Nearly half of all the world's plant species live in tropical forests.

MOUNTAINS

On the lower slopes of high mountains, there is conifer forest as far up as the "tree line." Above this line, there are grassy meadows, shrubby heaths, or bogs.

FRESHWATER

Lakes, ponds, rivers, and streams are full of rainwater on its way back to the sea. This freshwater is an important habitat for a wide variety of plants and animals.

OCEANS

Saltwater seas cover most of the Earth. Here, the Sun's energy is harvested by tiny floating creatures called plankton. Near the coasts are coral reefs or seaweed forests.

POLAR REGIONS

White, dry as a **desert**, and dark for *half the year*, the polar regions are some of the most **extreme** places on Earth.

POLAR REGIONS

And they are also the most fragile, warming twice as fast as the tropics. In these vulnerable places, changing climate is affecting the plants, animals, and people that live there. These areas are of special importance to the world and we need to do all we can to protect them.

where on earth...?

With months of endless darkness, hurricane winds, and freezing temperatures, the poles really are vast, frozen wildernesses. Yet plants and animals thrive here and have become so good at living in the "freezer" that they probably could not survive anywhere else. They like it cold!

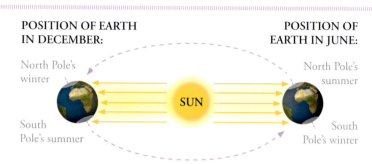

POSITION OF EARTH IN DECEMBER:

POSITION OF EARTH IN JUNE:

North Pole's winter

South Pole's summer

North Pole's summer

South Pole's winter

SUN

The Arctic and Antarctic have seasons at opposite times of the year. From this diagram you can see that during both places' winters, they receive no sunlight at all.

THE ARCTIC
—frozen sea surrounded by land at the top of the Earth

Six countries own different parts of the Arctic—Greenland, Russian Federation, Norway, Finland, Canada, and the United States. The US bought a part of the Arctic (Alaska) from Russia in 1867 for $7.2 million (approximately $135 million in today's money), and it became a US state in 1959.

The coldest temperature of a place inhabited by people was recorded in Siberia in the Arctic: -90.4°F (-68°C)—plus windchill!

PACIFIC OCEAN

Russian Federation

NORTH AMERICA

ASIA

NORTH POLE

Canada

The Arctic border

Greenland

Approximately four million people live in the Arctic (as opposed to about 4,000 seasonal researchers who stay on Antarctica).

ATLANTIC OCEAN

EUROPE

What is the Arctic? Most of the Arctic is taken up by the frozen Arctic Ocean. The central part, around the North Pole, is frozen solid all year round, but the outer edges thaw and break up in summer. The Arctic also includes land, at the edges of which is a treeless landscape called tundra.

WHY SO COLD?

Because Earth has a curved surface, the poles receive 20% less sunlight than the tropics at the equator. While the Sun shines overhead at the tropics, it is always low in the sky at the poles. At such a shallow angle, its rays have to cut across more of Earth's atmosphere, so less energy gets through. In addition to this, fierce, freezing gales make heat disappear more quickly: "wind chill," as this is known, makes -54°F (-48°C) feel like -93°F (-69°C). The center of Antarctica is on average much colder than the Arctic for two reasons: it's higher with more mountains, and it's farther from the warming waters of the ocean.

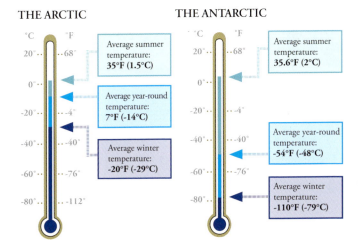

THE ARCTIC

Average summer temperature: 35°F (1.5°C)

Average year-round temperature: 7°F (-14°C)

Average winter temperature: -20°F (-29°C)

THE ANTARCTIC

Average summer temperature: 35.6°F (2°C)

Average year-round temperature: -54°F (-48°C)

Average winter temperature: -110°F (-79°C)

CHALLENGING CLIMATE

Life at the poles is a fight for survival. At both poles, the meager sunlight means there is little energy for plants to grow and little food for animals. There is not enough energy to make trees grow and, without them, there is no shelter from blistering winds. In this harsh environment, animals rush to breed in the brief respite of summer. For everything else, the pace of life is more relaxed. In the slow-motion Arctic, some caterpillars take 14 years to become moths.

Arctic caterpillar, Alaska

AFRICA

ATLANTIC OCEAN

INDIAN OCEAN

SOUTH AMERICA

SOUTH POLE

Antarctica is the world's driest desert; in some places it has not rained or snowed for centuries.

ANTARCTICA
—frozen land surrounded by sea at the bottom of the Earth

Antarctica is the only continent on Earth dedicated to peaceful scientific cooperation, "for the benefit of all mankind," by virtue of the Antarctic Treaty, signed in December 1959. The continent is not "owned" by any country.

PACIFIC OCEAN

The coldest temperature recorded was -128.6°F (-89.2°C) in 1983.

What time is it? This is a tricky question in Antarctica where all time zones meet. So people there use New Zealand time.

New Zealand

AUSTRALIA

What is Antarctica? The region around the South Pole, Antarctica, is the coldest place on Earth. While the Arctic is a flat, frozen ocean surrounded by land, Antarctica is the opposite, a frozen mountainous continent, surrounded by ocean. The only land animals in this freezing desert are penguins and seals.

the high arctic

The Arctic has two very different ecosystems. At the extreme north, there is a world of sea ice dominated by a few marine mammals, such as polar bears, whales, walruses, and seals. This is known as the "high Arctic." Farther south, the warmer, sunnier tundra has a richer ecosystem and is home to many more species of animals, birds, insects, and plants. Although most Arctic species are adapted for life on either the ice cap or the tundra, some—including polar bears—will range between both.

ARCTIC OWLS
Also known as snowy owls, these birds are found throughout the Arctic. Males are white, while females are mottled. They feed on lemmings.

Arctic hares in the high Arctic stay white all year, so the snow camouflages them. Their ear tips are black, perhaps to absorb sunlight and keep their ears warm.

Dog sleighs are the traditional way Arctic people get around on the ice.

Close to nature In the Arctic, humans are closely linked to the ecosystem and the animals that live there. They only thrive if the Arctic animals are thriving.

Watch out for polar bears! Signs like this in the inhabited part of the Arctic warn people that there could be polar bears around.

ICE FOX
The Arctic fox lives farther north than any other fox. It also has the warmest fur of any mammal, including the polar bear. These foxes hunt lemmings, but will eat any leftovers they find as well.

A world of ice Ice dominates the Arctic. During winter, the North Pole sees no sunlight at all for six months. That is why a large area around the Pole remains permanently frozen. Farther south, there is more sunlight and it is warmer. Here, the solid ice is frozen in winter, but thinner and more broken-up (or completely melted) in summer.

The Arctic food web The ocean is a vital part of the Arctic, creating the marine food web on which its ecosystem depends. The food web is fueled by energy harnessed from the Sun by tiny microscopic creatures. The energy is carried right up to the polar bears, and the top predator—man.

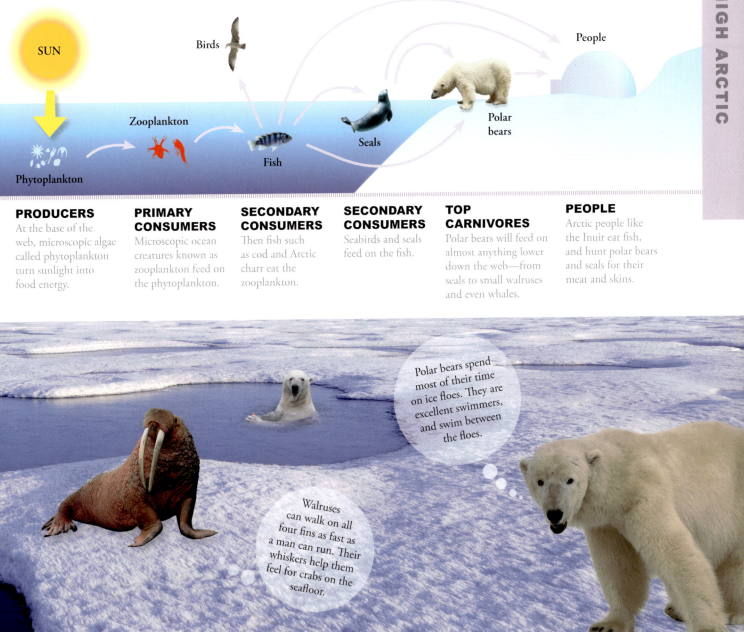

SUN

Birds

People

Zooplankton

Phytoplankton

Fish

Seals

Polar bears

PRODUCERS
At the base of the web, microscopic algae called phytoplankton turn sunlight into food energy.

PRIMARY CONSUMERS
Microscopic ocean creatures known as zooplankton feed on the phytoplankton.

SECONDARY CONSUMERS
Then fish such as cod and Arctic charr eat the zooplankton.

SECONDARY CONSUMERS
Seabirds and seals feed on the fish.

TOP CARNIVORES
Polar bears will feed on almost anything lower down the web—from seals to small walruses and even whales.

PEOPLE
Arctic people like the Inuit eat fish, and hunt polar bears and seals for their meat and skins.

Polar bears spend most of their time on ice floes. They are excellent swimmers, and swim between the floes.

Walruses can walk on all four fins as fast as a man can run. Their whiskers help them feel for crabs on the seafloor.

ARCTIC "RABBITS"
Lemmings live in Northern Canada and are an important part of the food chain there. They make burrows in the snow where they are safe from the cold and wind.

HOLE MAINTENANCE
In fall and early winter, holes in the ice start freezing over, so seals create breathing holes. They keep the holes open with their strong claws, and by pushing their noses through.

SUMMER VEGETATION
It is hard for plants to grow in the Arctic. Even in the summer it is cold and windy. Yet, many types of plants have adapted to Arctic life by growing low to the ground.

FUR COATS
In the high Arctic, people still live by hunting seals for food and clothing. Some still use traditional sleds pulled by dogs, but most now use snowmobiles.

melting arctic

People are worried about global warming everywhere on Earth, but the poles are giving most cause for concern. The Arctic is warming *twice as quickly* as the world average and both the ice cap and the tundra farther south are beginning to melt. Scientists think the Arctic may **lose** almost all its **summer sea ice** within decades.

1979

2007

The area of Arctic sea ice has been shrinking by about 0.7% each year for several decades.

By 2007, the area of Arctic sea ice had plummeted to a 29-year low.

These images show the yearly minimum area of ice, which occurs each year in summer, between September and October.

Sea levels could rise by 3 ft (1 m) by 2100,

Threatened animals An Arctic with less ice would be a different place. Polar bears hunt on the pack ice and use ice floes as stepping stones to move around. Seals and walruses give birth on ice and rest there when they are not in the water. In a warmer Arctic, these animals could become extinct.

Glaciers Apart from the ice cap, there are huge glaciers in the continents farther south: frozen rivers of ice that snake down through mountains in places such as Greenland and Norway. When the Arctic heats up, the glaciers will also start to melt and drain into the sea, further adding to the problem.

Industry The gas and oil industry in the Arctic causes pollution and has brought new settlers to the Arctic, turning native people into small minorities in their traditional areas. Reduced sea ice could increase marine transportation and access to natural resources, making oil spills more likely.

Local changes, global effects Sea-level rises caused by melting polar ice will cause more flooding in coastal areas around the world. Extreme floods currently happen in low-lying New York City once a century. But if sea levels were 3 ft (1 m) higher, floods could happen every three years. The melting Arctic will bring a worrying change. Currently, the icy white poles reflect most sunlight back into space, keeping the planet cooler. But as the ice disappears, more of the Sun's heat will be absorbed instead. Earth will warm more quickly—and climate change may accelerate.

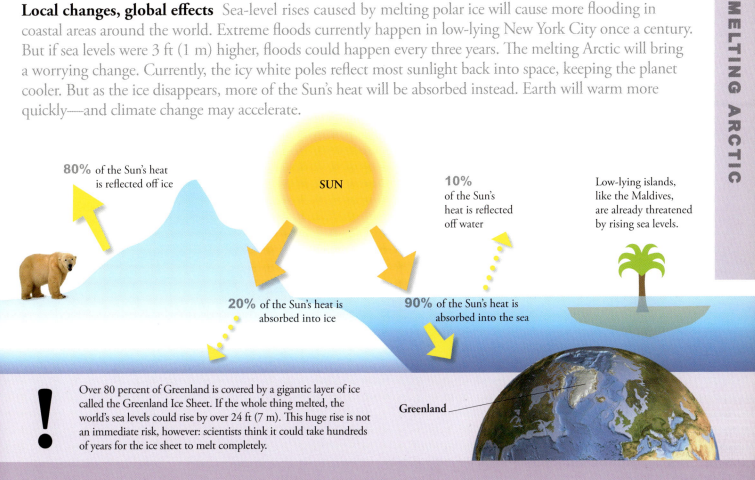

80% of the Sun's heat is reflected off ice

SUN

10% of the Sun's heat is reflected off water

Low-lying islands, like the Maldives, are already threatened by rising sea levels.

20% of the Sun's heat is absorbed into ice

90% of the Sun's heat is absorbed into the sea

! Over 80 percent of Greenland is covered by a gigantic layer of ice called the Greenland Ice Sheet. If the whole thing melted, the world's sea levels could rise by over 24 ft (7 m). This huge rise is not an immediate risk, however: scientists think it could take hundreds of years for the ice sheet to melt completely.

Greenland

partly due to Greenland ice starting to melt.

Tourism Tourist cruises are gaining better access to the frozen north, bringing disturbance, litter, and pollution with them. But the wilderness they come to see may have long gone.

Native people If seals disappear, what would happen to the Inuit hunters who depend on them for food? To hunt, catch, and share ringed seals is their way of life.

The fierce Sun Arctic people have noticed that the Sun's heat feels "stronger, stinging, and sharp." Sunburn and strange skin rashes never experienced before are becoming common. This is due to too much ultraviolet radiation from the Sun penetrating the thin ozone layer over the Arctic.

 With the sea ice and permafrost melting, the Inuit of the Arctic face an uncertain future. Find out more about their lives and culture at: www.athropolis.com/links/inuit.htm

the polar bear

THESE ULTIMATE ARCTIC WARRIORS, FOUND AS FAR NORTH AS THE POLE ITSELF, ARE THREATENED BY THE MELTING ICE CAP

Ice is vital for polar bears. They hunt seals on it, eat on it, and use it like a bridge to move from one part of the frozen ocean to another. But now the Arctic ice is threatened by global warming, polar bears are threatened, too. Summer comes sooner, so the ice melts earlier and the bears have less time to feed. They put on less weight for the winter and therefore have less chance of survival. Already polar bears are being seen in poor condition and the average weight and number of cubs has declined. Now that there is less ice and more water, the bears are having to swim farther. An Arctic without polar bears seems unthinkable, but there are fewer than 25,000 bears left worldwide. They are becoming a threatened species and may disappear entirely if global warming trends continue.

See this website to learn more about polar bears and how they are being protected by the World Wildlife Fund: www.worldwildlife.org/polarbears

Polar bears live in the Arctic and the very north of Canada. The effects of global warming can be seen in the declining number of cubs being born.

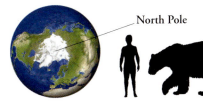

North Pole

Polar bears hunt ice-dwelling ringed seals. The seals have also been affected by the rise in temperatures as the snow caves in which they rear pups are melting earlier. Fewer seals means less food for the bears.

A warm coat The polar bear is wonderfully adapted to the harsh conditions of its home. Its coat is about 10 times thicker than a person's winter overcoat. And underneath that there is another 4 in (10 cm) of fatty blubber to insulate bears when they swim in the freezing Arctic waters. One of a polar bear's biggest problems is overheating, which is why bears move so slowly and rest often.

tundra ecosystem

Between the icy wastelands of the Arctic north and the forest biomes farther south there is a swathe of in-between territory called tundra. Tundra is too cold for trees to grow, aside from a few dwarf species at its southern edges. Tundra covers four percent of the Earth's surface.

JAN	FEB	MAR	APRIL	MAY	JUNE	JULY	AUG	SEPT	OCT	NOV	DEC
3	8	12	15	19	24	24	18	14	11	6	2

HOURS OF DAYLIGHT IN LAPLAND (average per day)
During most of the year the tundra is bitingly cold and windy. The winter is long and dark with only a few hours of light each day. In the brief warm summer, when it is daylight almost continuously, life takes off.

TO THE **NORTH** Arctic ice cap

N

S

TO THE **SOUTH** boreal forests

What is permafrost?
Tundra is built on frozen soil called permafrost, which lies 20 in (50 cm) beneath the surface. Above it is an active layer of soil that thaws in summer and freezes in winter.

Bright buttercups, poppies, and sedges, as well as mosses and grasses, cover the tundra in summer.

SUNBATHING
Sulfur butterflies almost always stand with their folded wings side-on to the Sun so they can absorb the maximum amount of solar energy.

How the animals cope The tundra is a biome with a very cold climate, hardly any rain, and a short growing season. Plants are low-growing to escape the wind, and flowers turn their faces to track the Sun. Animals are adapted to long, cold winters and breed and raise young quickly in the short summer. Many birds are migrants that come to breed and then fly somewhere warmer.

Tundra food web

Food is more limited at the poles than anywhere else on Earth. Creatures compete to survive, but the fate of each one depends on all the others.

Snow goose

Arctic fox

Lemming

Snowy owl

Grizzly bear

Fungus

SUN AIR WATER

Caribou

Wolf

PRODUCERS
Plants use sunlight to turn air, water, and nutrients into food, ultimately fueling everything else on the tundra.

PRIMARY CONSUMERS
The next link in the chain are herbivores, which eat plants. They include caribou, geese, lemmings, and grouse.

SECONDARY CONSUMERS
Secondary consumers are carnivores, living off primary consumers. They include wolves, foxes, owls, and insect-eating animals.

TOP CARNIVORES
Grizzly bears eat plants and berries in season. They will also eat whatever meat is available including moose, caribou, hare, and fish.

DECOMPOSERS
Fungi and miscroscopic organisms break down dead matter and waste, returning it to the soil so the cycle can begin again.

Caribou put on weight in summer, eating plants, berries, and mushrooms.

FUR AND FLEECE
An ice-age survivor, the musk ox has the ultimate fur coat and can stay out all winter. It's the only animal that never needs shelter. Reintroductions to the wild have boosted numbers.

MOSQUITO BITES
Huge swarms of mosquitoes thrive in the shallow lakes of the tundra. They come out in early summer and bite animals and birds. Caribou are particular favorites.

SUMMER VACATION
The Arctic tern visits the tundra in summer to breed and then flies south to catch another summer in Antarctica. It sees more daylight than any other animal on Earth.

CARIBOU FOOD
Lichens, made up of fungi living with algae, are an important part of the tundra vegetation. Caribou are able to eat lichen because they produce a special enzyme that helps them digest it.

warming tundra

Some areas of tundra have **warmed faster** than almost **anywhere else** on Earth, with an average temperature increase of 5.4°F (3°C) in the last 40 years. This is thought to be caused by a combination of man-made *climate change* and melting ice exposing more bare ground, which warms up more quickly than **snow** and **ice**.

- ■ Current permafrost area
- ■ Projected permafrost area (2100)
- □ Current sea ice

Projected change in Arctic permafrost by 2100

A thawing permafrost not only affects

Keeping it cool The Trans-Alaska pipeline was raised above the ground for 400 miles (640 km) of its length to stop it from transferring heat onto the ground and thawing the permafrost. It is likely that as the ground becomes more unstable, maintenance costs will rise.

Cracking up The thawing permafrost also causes problems to buildings. This house in Siberia was built on hard, frozen ground, but as it melts, the building moves. The same problem occurs to Siberian railroad tracks, runways, and other important infrastructure.

End of the road As the permafrost thaws, the number of days each year that ice roads and tundra are frozen solid enough to travel on decreases. In Alaska this is now just under 80 days a year. Further disruption for transportation and industry on land seem likely.

Methane alert Siberia's peat bogs have been producing methane since they were formed at the end of the last ice age, but most of the gas is trapped in the permafrost. As the bogs thaw, they may release billions of tons of methane into the atmosphere.

Present sources of methane in the atmosphere:

about 55% is due to human activity (farming and rotting waste)

about 8% is from other natural sources

about 37% is released from wetlands

Methane as a greenhouse gas Methane makes up 13% of greenhouse gases. It stays in the atmosphere for only eight years or so, but traps 23 times more heat than carbon dioxide. Carbon dioxide is currently the biggest cause of global warming, but methane is important, too.

the tundra, but also Earth's atmosphere.

Shifting northward As temperatures rise, the depth of the layer that thaws each year is increasing in many areas. The southern limit of permafrost will shrink and shift northward several hundred miles during this century, reducing the tundra's extent.

Pools in the permafrost In summer the layer of frozen soil keeps melting snow and ice from draining away. Over the surface, marshy pools and shallow lakes form. Widespread thawing will cause lakes to drain in some places and create new wetlands in other areas.

Life on frozen ground In Russia alone, 200,000 people live for part of the year as nomads, herding reindeer. Thawing permafrost means there are likely to be fewer reindeer and as a result the nomads will find it harder to survive too.

the caribou

CHANGING CONDITIONS IN THE TUNDRA ARE AFFECTING HOW CARIBOU HERDS FIND FOOD AND RAISE CALVES

Caribou are found in northern North America, Greenland, and across northern Europe and northern Asia.

Tundra

Many Arctic peoples in Europe and Asia still herd caribou. They eat their meat and use their skins to make tents and warm clothes.

In some places, global warming is leading to heavier snow and rain. This freezes solid over the deer's main food—lichen.

Deer known as caribou in North America and reindeer in northern Europe migrate between their winter home in the cold forests and their summer home on the tundra. They depend on the tundra; anything that threatens it, threatens them, too. As the tundra warms and disappears, caribou lose their calving and feeding grounds, and their numbers decline. River ice is thawing earlier in spring so some rivers are no longer frozen when the caribou come to cross them. For the porcupine caribou herd in the Yukon in northern Canada, this has led to the mass drowning of newborn calves. In the fall, conditions that alternate between freezing and thawing cover the deer's food with ice that is too thick to break with their hooves.

antarctic ecosystem

Antarctica is Earth's last great wilderness: a land of rock and ice far from civilization. A cold ocean current, called the polar front, cuts off the Antarctic continent from the tropical waters and warmer lands above. Isolated and barren, this place is full of extremes. There are mountains as high as the Alps and even the smaller peaks are buried under several miles of ice. Three-quarters of the world's freshwater is locked up here in a massive ice sheet that's bigger than the United States.

17 species of penguin visit Antarctica each year, including this king penguin and its chicks.

Giant petrel

Out of those 17 species only the emperor, the Adelie, and the chinstrap make their homes there, braving the harsh winter.

A harsh place to live Over 98 percent of Antarctica is covered by ice, which makes life hard for mammals. The only animals that live here for the whole year are penguins and seals.

Krill are the most numerous animals on Earth.

THE KRILL CONNECTION
Perhaps the most important Antarctic species is krill. Krill are like shrimps. They form the bridge in the food chain between microscopic organisms and fish, birds, and mammals.

Land, sea, air Antarctica is essentially one big habitat: a huge rocky ice rink that doubles in size when the ocean freezes each winter. An Antarctic winter is like nothing else on Earth: little can survive in this cold, rainless, and windy desert. In summer, it bursts into life. On land, millions of penguins, seals, and seabirds arrive to breed, and under water in the Antarctic ocean, sea life thrives.

The Antarctic Treaty Antarctica is a very special place where science has top priority. The only people who live in this ecosystem are scientists. No single country owns Antarctica, but 46 member countries are currently signed up. Below is what they signed up to:

The 2nd Amundsen Scott station

Scientists can live and work in this station throughout the year.

- Antarctica may only be used for peaceful purposes
- Scientific information must be freely exchanged
- Free access for all nations
- Military explosions and disposal of nuclear waste are prohibited
- No territorial claims can be made while the treaty is in place

All Antarctic whale species migrate long distances, feeding in the cold, nutrient-rich Antarctic Ocean during the summer then heading north to breed and give birth to their young during the winter months.

Walruses breed on ice-free islands with easy access to the sea.

SEAL TEETH
Weddell seals use their teeth to keep open "trap doors" in the ice. Eventually, the ice grinds down their teeth so much that they cannot chew food, and they die.

PINK SNOW
Algae in the ice bloom, turning ice caves pink. The pigments (color chemicals) in the algae capture light to make energy via photosynthesis, while the snow provides moisture.

WHALE SPOTTING
Many whales visit Antarctica including the humpback whale, (below) and minke whale. They come to feast on the abundant krill.

UNDER THE ICE
Beneath the ice, the warmer Antarctic ocean is packed with everything from microscopic bugs and plankton to squid, jellyfish, and starfish.

threatened antarctica

The South Pole is about 2,200 miles (3,500 km) from South America, the nearest continent (a vast distance slightly less than the width of the United States). Although this is an incredibly **remote** region—one of the only places where people have never settled—it is still **threatened** by human activities. Most of the threats to Antarctica, including *global warming* and *pollution*, are caused by things people are doing far away.

Ninety percent of the world's ice is

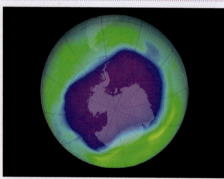

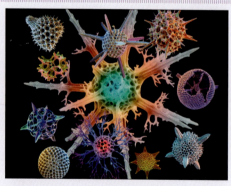

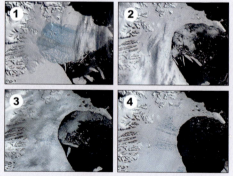

Ozone hole In 1985, scientists noticed a huge hole in the ozone layer over Antarctica. The ozone layer screens out ultraviolet radiation from the Sun. The chemicals chlorofluorocarbons (CFCs) were to blame and so most countries began to phase them out. The hole is expected to disappear by about 2050.

UV affects plankton Harmful ultraviolet rays can stop phytoplankton from growing properly. Phytoplanktons are the staple diet of krill, which in turn are eaten by the penguins, seals, and seabirds that breed in Antarctica. The hole in the ozone therefore threatens the Antarctic food web from the bottom up.

Melting ice Huge chunks of ice are falling into the sea due to global warming. This series of pictures shows the collapse of the Larsen B ice shelf. An area of ice 720 ft (220 m) thick and 1,255 sq miles (3,250 sq km) in size broke off. The ice, which had been in place for 12,000 years, took just 35 days to disappear.

A chemical mix Chemicals people pour into rivers or seas can be swept around the world by ocean currents, eventually washing up at the poles. Or they can be blown away with air pollution and fall onto Antarctica with snow. Scientists have found traces of harmful chemicals in Antarctic penguins, seals, whales, and seabirds. The chemicals include long-banned deadly pesticides such as DDTs.

Minimize pollution— and never throw any garbage on the ground, at the beach, in the river, or in the sea!

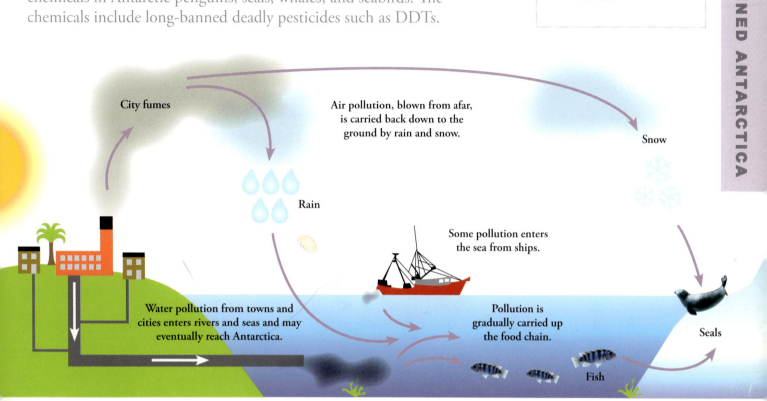

City fumes

Air pollution, blown from afar, is carried back down to the ground by rain and snow.

Snow

Rain

Some pollution enters the sea from ships.

Water pollution from towns and cities enters rivers and seas and may eventually reach Antarctica.

Pollution is gradually carried up the food chain.

Seals

Fish

locked in freezing Antarctica.

Oil mining Antarctica has been designated "a natural reserve dedicated to peace and to society" and nations have agreed not to explore for minerals or oil under the terms of the Antarctic Treaty. But as supplies of Earth's resources dwindle elsewhere, a time may come when it makes economic sense to develop Antarctica too.

Rising krill catches Antarctic krill form dense concentrations in summer that can be several miles across and 65 ft (20 m) deep. These have attracted fishing fleets hoping to make krill a food for humans. Current catch levels are rising, but are not at a dangerous level yet.

Whaling Whale hunting in the 19th century reduced the numbers of most species to the point where there were too few to hunt. Blue whales are at less than one percent of their original numbers and are still not increasing despite years of protection. Now the whale fleets are setting off again...

emperor **penguins**

EMPEROR PENGUIN NUMBERS ARE GOING DOWN AS THEIR FOOD SUPPLY IS AFFECTED BY GLOBAL WARMING

Huddling in the cold and waddling on ice, diving through waves and tobogganing through snow, penguins are the icons of Antarctica. Of the 50 million or so penguins in Antarctica, only emperor penguins breed on the ice and snow. They are the ultimate polar survivors, breeding farther south than any other animal. And they are perfectly adapted for the task. However, as Antarctica warms due to global warming, there will be less ice in the sea from one year to the next. This affects the food chain as reduced ice means reduced sea-ice algae (a major food for krill). This leads to fewer krill, which is the penguins' staple diet. Less food means fewer emperor penguins. Over the past 50 years, the population of Antarctic emperor penguins has declined by 50 percent.

There are at least 40 different colonies of emperor penguins in the Antarctic. Some colonies comprise no more than 200 pairs, while the biggest ones can consist of more than 50,000 pairs.

Antarctica

Much of a penguin's life is taken up with long feeding trips to the sea. They can't fly, so they have to waddle over rocks and skid down the ice instead. Their curved bodies make great toboggans, using their flippers to push along. In the water, they whizz along at up to 6 mph (10 km/h)—slightly faster than Olympic swimmers.

A challenge to breed Emperor penguins court and mate quickly, taking advantage of the short Antarctic summer. After six weeks the female lays a single egg, then passes it to the male. He takes over while the female makes a 60-mile (100-km) trip to the sea for food. As winter sets in, he huddles with other males in the windy cold, cradling the egg on his feet. Nine weeks later, in the constant darkness of an Antarctic winter, the chick hatches and the females miraculously reappear with food.

MAKING A DIFFERENCE

Walk to school—whatever the weather!

Garbage in the waterways

The world's waterways are all connected by Earth's seas and oceans. A plastic bag in a river in England could end up in the Arctic. There it could be eaten by a sea bird or animal. What can you do?

1. **Take part** in **beach** or **river clean-ups**, or organize your own local clean-up. Try to get your school involved.

2. **Pick up** any litter and put it in the **TRASH**.

Arctic Research Assistant needed

Are you ready for a new challenge?

- **Most important** Must be passionate about the polar regions.
- **The job** Taking ice samples, temperature recordings, examining data, monitoring wildlife, and other outdoor work.
- **The environment** Extremely cold. Long, dark winters.
- **The successful applicant** You'll need a good sense of humor, to be able to work well as part of a team, and mix easily with people from different backgrounds, countries, and ages.
- **On the menu** Fishsticks

What can we do to make a difference to the poles? Even though they are far away, we can do things to help.

KNOW THE DEBATE

developing
the polar regions

- **Fishing around Antarctica**—the opportunities for fishing are immense (and stocks elsewhere are dwindling). Fishing could be limited and catches strictly monitored.
- **Tourism**—visitors will help native people earn a living, and the more people that see the area, the more it will be in their memories as a place to treasure.
- **A treasure trove of minerals**—mining could be done in a way that makes as little impact on the environment as possible. If people care about the Arctic and Antarctica, customers won't put up with companies that ruin it.
- **Drilling for oil**—as world resources of oil dry up, oil in the Arctic and Antarctica provide an answer. Again, the extraction process could be done with sensitivity to the environment, and could be carefully monitored.
- **In return for a license** to mine resources, companies could put money into science projects, vital to us all.

protecting
the polar regions

- Squid, krill, and fish form the base of the food chain so fishing quotas must not be increased.
- **Mining companies have historically been destructive** to the environment. They pollute and destroy habitat.
- The dumping of industrial waste in the Arctic **causes long-term pollution** and enters the food chain.
- **Tourism is destructive** and polluting. Garbage dropped in freezing temperatures never biodegrades (breaks down).
- Scientists from over 25 countries have proved the **importance of Antarctica in learning about life on Earth.**
- **Better to play safe,** than be sorry later.
- **The Antarctic Treaty proves nations can work together for the good of all mankind.** Let's leave it that way.

Dear Congressman Black,

I am concerned about the polar regions. The ice is melting due to global warming. Animals, including polar bears and penguins, are losing their habitat. Fishing in the Arctic Ocean is endangering fish stocks, and mining for oil and minerals is also harmful.

We really need to act now to protect these special places.

Please make decisions that will bring an end to global warming and do all you can to inform people of the problems at the poles that could affect everyone.

Sincerely,

Alex Potter

Start lobbying

Write a letter to the government to show that you care!

what you can do

Political lobbying sounds complicated. But anyone can do it! Just find out your congress-person's or senators' names and addresses and write letters. Find the senators from your state at www.senate.gov.

TEMPERATE FORESTS

The world's **temperate forests** lie roughly between the *poles* and the *equator*.

The word temperate means "not extreme." The temperate regions on Earth lie in the middle latitudes, where there are distinct warm and cold seasons that we call summer and winter. Trees thrive in these areas, as long as there's enough rainfall, and forests nurture a wondrous variety of animals and plants.

TEMPERATE FORESTS

where on earth...?

Forests grow wherever in the world it's warm and wet enough for trees to thrive. Temperate forests grow in places where there is precipitation (rain and snow) throughout the year, but separate warm and cold seasons.

KEY

- Coniferous Forest
- Deciduous Forest
- Temperate Rain forest
- Mediterranean Scrub

NORTH AMERICA

SOUTH AMERICA

In mature forests, the **BIGGEST** trees are usually more than 100 years old.

Many temperate-forest trees are now showing worrying signs of **DIEBACK**, which may be a direct result of climate change.

Temperate summers are never as hot as the **TROPICS**, and winters are never as cold as the **POLES**.

TYPES OF FOREST

● **CONIFEROUS FOREST**
Conifer trees have cones and needles instead of leaves. They are found where it is warm enough for trees to grow for a few months each year. In the far north, conifer forests are called boreal forests.

● **DECIDUOUS FOREST**
Deciduous trees have leaves—very few have needles. Where summers are warm and winters are mild, deciduous trees drop their leaves for the winter and grow them again in the spring.

● **TEMPERATE RAIN FOREST**
On the Pacific coast of North America, the climate is mild and wet. Here, there are tall, wide conifers covered in moss. These lush forests, and others like them, are called temperate rain forests.

● **MEDITERRANEAN SCRUB**
Shrubs and trees in this type of forest keep their leaves all year long. They are especially adapted to survive hot, dry summers, and to make the most of cool, moist winters.

Rooted to the spot Once a tree has taken root, it has to stand in the same place for the rest of its life. If the weather changes, or conditions become unsuitable, trees can't do anything about it, and they suffer stress.

SEASONS SHIFT
The seasonal change in temperature is a challenge for animals and plants. Their coping strategies, like hibernating in winter or flowering in spring, are timed to match the seasons, but the seasons are changing.

ON THE MOVE
As our climate warms up, ideal conditions for each species are moving toward the poles. Mobile creatures like birds can move easily, but temperate forests will have to move too, and they can't travel quickly.

CARBON STORES
Trees absorb and store carbon. Temperate rain forests store more carbon per acre (hectare) than any other land habitat. If they die, their carbon will add to the greenhouse gases.

ANCIENT WOODS
There have been conifers on the Earth for 300 million years—they once extended into the Arctic. Deciduous forests are a little more recent—they have been around for 65 million years.

LATE ARRIVAL
Compared to the other forests, Mediterranean scrub is relatively modern, arriving over the last 40 million years. Much of its wildlife is unique to each continent, because it evolved in isolation.

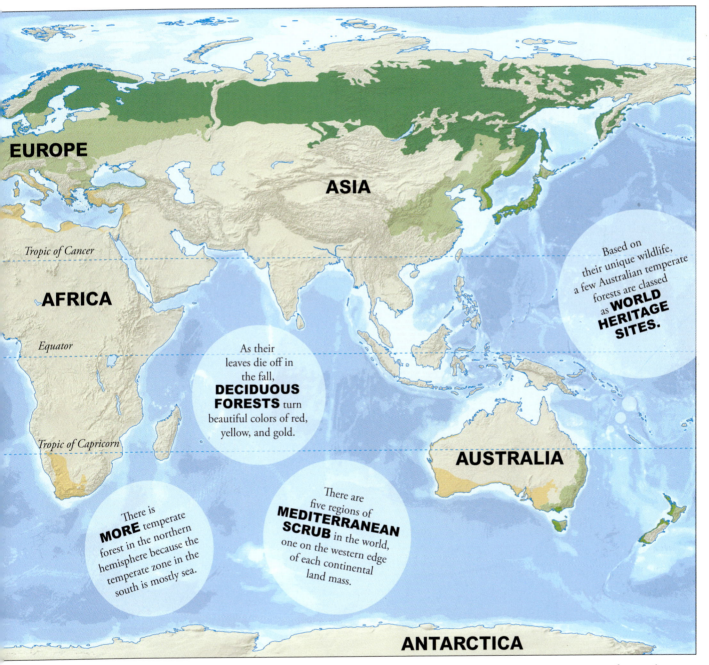

EUROPE

ASIA

AFRICA

Tropic of Cancer

Equator

Tropic of Capricorn

Based on their unique wildlife, a few Australian temperate forests are classed as **WORLD HERITAGE SITES.**

As their leaves die off in the fall, **DECIDUOUS FORESTS** turn beautiful colors of red, yellow, and gold.

AUSTRALIA

There is **MORE** temperate forest in the northern hemisphere because the temperate zone in the south is mostly sea.

There are five regions of **MEDITERRANEAN SCRUB** in the world, one on the western edge of each continental land mass.

ANTARCTICA

When this happens year after year, trees are vulnerable to attack by disease and insects. Branches and shoots die (called "dieback") and sometimes the whole tree is killed. Often, this is triggered by summer drought, a sign of climate change.

One reason trees are so important is that other wildlife depends on them—mosses, ferns, and funguses, bugs, beetles, wasps, caterpillars, birds, snakes, and squirrels all live on, or in, the bark, leaves, and branches of trees.

boreal ecosystem

Boreal forest, also called the taiga, is named after Boreas, Greek God of the north wind. Made up of conifer trees, it's the world's largest biome on land, covering 17 percent of Earth's vegetated land surface (more than 5,800,000 sq miles/ 15 million sq km), circling the planet in the northern hemisphere. The growing season, when there's enough warmth and sunlight for plants to grow, lasts just two or three months, and the winters are long and frozen. Average winter temperatures often fall to a bitter -22°F(-30°C).

Patches of soil underneath the northern boreal forest are permanently frozen—this is called permafrost.

Moose have very long legs so they can wade in boreal-forest lakes.

Trees are mainly spruce, pine, and fir, which have needles all year round. In Siberia, there are lots of larch, a type of conifer that sheds its needles in winter.

Some species, like the moose, the Siberian tit, and the great gray owl, are found in all the world's boreal forests. Others live only on one or two continents—the snowshoe hare, for example, is found only in America, and the Siberian tiger is found only in Europe and Asia. The red squirrel, and many songbirds, have similar American and European versions.

BERRY BUSHES
The berries of small plants like bilberry and cowberry in Europe, and blueberry and bunchberry in North America, provide vital food for birds and mammals, including bears.

TIGER OF THE TAIGA
In the Russian far east, two rare cats prowl boreal forests. Siberian (Amur) tigers and Amur leopards both have long thick fur, long legs, and big feet to survive the months of snow.

The need for needles

Because they have needles all year round, conifer trees waste none of the precious growing season producing new ones, so the trees can start growing new wood as soon as it's warm. Eventually, all needles do fall off and decay, creating a thick spongy carpet on the forest floor. Waxy and full of sticky resin, they rot slowly in the freezing temperatures. Acids are washed out of them into the soil. Mosses thrive on this shady, acidic ground, but few other plants survive.

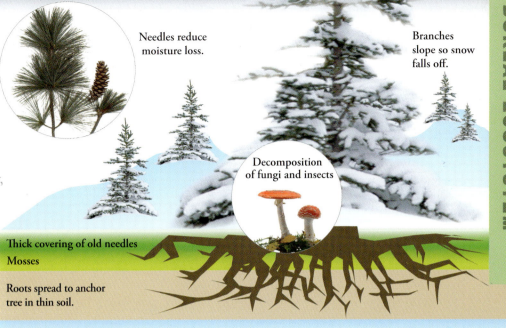

Needles reduce moisture loss.

Branches slope so snow falls off.

Decomposition of fungi and insects

Thick covering of old needles

Mosses

Roots spread to anchor tree in thin soil.

Permafrost in the far north

In winter, Arctic foxes come in two colors, white and "blue", which is a very grayish blue. In summer, they are brown with whitish bellies.

Arctic wolves are always pale in color—white, cream, or light gray.

FOREST FIRES

Most boreal forest fires happen naturally. They are a vital part of the ecosystem since they help to release seeds, and provide ashes that nourish small plants.

INSECT INVASIONS

Insects often invade the forest and strip the needles off older trees. Like fires, these insect attacks disturb the system, and are important for keeping a rich mix of tree species.

FOREST PEOPLE

At one time, native peoples lived in boreal forests. The Ojibway of North America built birch-bark wigwams as homes, dressed in furs, and even used moss as babies' nappies.

SAVING MOISTURE

Needles are narrow, tightly rolled leaves with a waxy coating. Because they don't lose much water by evaporation, needles stay in place through the very dry boreal winter when the water in the soil is frozen.

dying forest

Since **1970**, average temperatures in central **Siberia** (home to vast areas of boreal forests) have risen almost *3.5°F (2°C)*— nearly three times the global average. As upper layers of **permafrost** melt, more *water* runs off to the rivers, and the soil dries out. *Forest fires* are increasing. Stressed by **drier conditions**, trees succumb to insect attacks and die. But the forest cannot relocate fast enough to more suitable *places.*

Of all the world's forests, boreal forests

Insect invasion During the 1990s, the Kenai Peninsula had a devastating bark-beetle outbreak (more than 30 million trees died) as a result of unusually warm summers. Other insects can cause similarly dramatic damage (above, pine-beetle infestation).

Bark beetle

Spring's forward In Siberia, spring has arrived roughly a day earlier every year since 1982. In Alaska, spring starts two weeks earlier than it did in 1950. Warm springs trigger insect plagues and encourage birds like the northern wheatear (above) to migrate and breed earlier, causing problems in the food chain.

Fires burning Siberian forest fires (above) have increased tenfold in 20 years, and the area burned in North America has doubled. Global warming may be partly responsible, because it's made springs warmer, and summers drier. Scientists predict more fierce and frequent fires if carbon dioxide keeps pouring into the atmosphere.

Some experts have predicted a dramatic shrinking of the world's boreal forests (shown below, the Kenai Peninsula in Alaska). With climate change, ideal conditions for the boreal forest may move north 10 times faster than the forests can migrate. At the southern edge of the zone, fires will make it possible for a forest to convert to grassland fairly quickly. But at the northern edge, the trees will have to spread their seeds farther north to find suitable conditions, and this takes much longer. Unable to shift north, the total area of forest could shrink considerably.

are the most threatened by climate change.

Gold nugget

Gold leaf

Pulp factory Boreal forests are the world's pulp factories. More than 100 million trees are cut down every year, and between 33 and 50 percent of the wood ends up as paper. In Russia, only 14 percent of forests are now big enough to support the Siberian tiger, and only 10 percent of Canada's forests are protected.

Dangerous prospects Beneath the boreal forests, there are oil and gas deposits and valuable minerals like gold and diamonds. Prospecting and mining for these can devastate the forest. A patch of Canadian forest and peat bogs the size of Florida could soon be destroyed to mine oil in rocks known as tar sands.

Life at the edge At the southern edge, boreal forests often overlap deciduous forests. Since the 1980s, the trembling aspen, a common deciduous tree in many boreal forests (this one is in Colorado), has been suffering dieback caused by prolonged water shortages and insect invasions.

temperate rain forest

On the west coast of North America, between the sea and the Rocky Mountains, there's a very special kind of conifer forest called temperate rain forest. The weather is milder here than in boreal forest, and very wet, so the trees can keep growing for most of the year. They live for a long time and reach massive sizes, commonly 260 ft (80 m) high, with trunks 6–10 ft (2–3 m) across. In the dark, damp interior, the trees are draped with moss and supported by huge buttresses (trunks that spread out at the base like the legs of the Eiffel Tower).

Raccoons are curious creatures who will eat lots of different things, but they especially like catching fish and shellfish from the sea.

Temperate rain forests are wet, so forest fires are rare—they happen about once in 1,000 years. This is why the trees can get so old.

Red and green giants

The southern part of North America's rain forest is home to the famous California redwood trees (left). Some are over 2,200 years old, and the tallest-ever specimen is 367 ft (112 m) high. Even these giants are not as big as their South American cousins, the alerce trees of Chile's Valdivian forest, which can reach 374 ft (114 m)—some are over 3,000 years old. Now, since many alerce trees have been cut down for lumber, they are threatened with extinction.

DRIPPING FOGS

All year, fogs roll in from the sea and their moisture clings to the trees. California redwoods, which rely on these fogs for water, can only grow within 12 miles (20 km) of the coast.

ecosystem

Between mountains and sea Mountains keep temperate rain forests wet. Moist air from the ocean is forced up to pass over them. As it rises, it cools, and the moisture falls as rain. On the far side of the mountains, in what's called the "rain shadow," the weather is much drier. Coastal temperate rain forests are found in Norway, southern Chile, New Zealand, Tasmania, and Japan.

Moisture turns to rain.

SUN

The air is dry because its moisture has already fallen as rain.

Moist air from the ocean

Temperate rain forest

Rain shadow

Black bears climb trees. Mothers often leave their cubs in trees when they go off looking for food.

Native to North America, the bobcat has distinctive black stripes on its front legs, and a stubby tail that inspired its name.

LIFE-SAVING SPECIES
Native Americans used the leaves and branches of the Pacific yew as medicine, and modern scientists use its bark in a cancer drug. It takes three mature trees to treat one patient.

MYSTERY BIRD
Until 1974, no one could find the home of the marbled murrelet, a seabird of North America's west coast, because it nests in inland forests. As these disappear, its numbers decline.

THUNDERBIRD
At one time, many Native American cultures lived in fear of the legendary thunderbird, a giant godlike bird that lived in the mountains to the east and ate killer whales from the sea. People believed it could throw lightning, and make thunder by clapping its wings. The feared bird was often represented on carved totem poles.

HIDE AND SEEK
Unlike tropical rain forests, temperate rain forests are still and quiet, and the animals stay hidden. Most, like this Roosevelt elk, are brown and mottled or striped to blend into the forest shadows.

forest **and sea**

The glorious temperate rain forests of North America's west coast are nourished by the oceans alongside them, which are particularly rich in nutrients. Pacific salmon take these riches deep into the forests by swimming up rivers and streams in large numbers to mate and lay their eggs, or "spawn." These journeys are called salmon runs. Swimming up a single river, there can be 20 million fish. There are so many salmon that they make easy prey for grizzly bears. Normally solitary animals that only hunt at night, bears gather around streams and rivers at spawning time and stand in fast-flowing rapids to catch salmon as they leap. Getting past the bears is a dangerous game. In Alaska, grizzlies consume 40 percent of all sockeye salmon as they pass— there is such a glut that bears often take a single bite out of one salmon before discarding it and picking up another one.

Adult salmon live at sea. In late summer, when they have matured, they return to the place where they were born. There they spawn, then die.

The rotting carcasses are eaten by scavenging birds, which then fly over the forest, distributing valuable fertilizer in the form of droppings.

Salmon eggs

The next spring, the eggs hatch into young fish. These spend up to two years in freshwater before they head for the sea.

By eating salmon, bears transfer ocean nutrients such as nitrogen, potassium, and phosphorous, directly to the forest floor, feeding the trees. These are either in the form of bear droppings, or half-eaten fish carcasses dragged onto land. The dead fish are then devoured by maggots that carry the nutrients even farther in their own droppings when they grow into flies.

deciduous ecosystem

Warm temperate forests are found where there are obvious cold and warm seasons, but where precipitation (rain and snow) falls evenly throughout the year. There are large areas of this type of forest in Europe, North America, and Asia, and small patches in the southern hemisphere. Trees are mainly deciduous, which means they lose their leaves in the fall, and stand naked through winter. Common examples of deciduous trees are maple, beech, oak, and chestnut.

Summer temperature

Late-fall temperature

The big drop
In the fall, when temperatures fall and there is less light, the trees lose green chlorophyll from their leaves. The leaves turn brilliant shades of orange, red, and gold before they die and fall off.

Between 30 and 60 in (750 and 1,500 mm) of rain falls each year. Seasons are marked by differences in temperature, not precipitation. The growing season lasts about six months.

White admiral butterflies live in the deciduous woods of Europe and Asia. Their caterpillars feed on the leaves of woody climbers such as honeysuckle.

Deciduous means to "fall off naturally." In addition to leaves, ants' wings, deers' antlers, and children's teeth are all deciduous.

Living litter Dead leaves form a thick litter (a top layer of slightly decayed material) on the ground. Inside it, a rich community of invertebrates—worms, mites, and springtails—chew the leaves into tiny pieces. Microscopic bacteria and fungi continue to break them down so their nutrients are released for trees to use again.

FIT FOR A QUEEN
The nectar and pollen in spring woodland flowers are crucial for queen bumblebees, which are the only bees to survive the winter. All the others—males and female workers—die off in the fall, and queens found new colonies alone.

Deciduous forest food chain
Small birds, insects, and small mammals live off plants; larger birds and mammals eat insects and smaller birds and mammals; and top predators eat lots of other creatures.

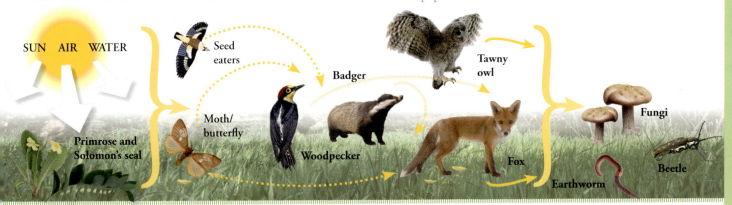

SUN AIR WATER

Primrose and Solomon's seal

Seed eaters

Moth/ butterfly

Badger

Woodpecker

Tawny owl

Fox

Fungi

Earthworm

Beetle

PRODUCERS
At the bottom of the deciduous food chain are a variety of trees, flowers, and large, tufty woodland grasses.

PRIMARY CONSUMERS
Moth and butterfly caterpillars eat tree leaves, while birds and squirrels eat seeds and nuts.

SECONDARY CONSUMERS
Woodpeckers eat insects and caterpillars, and badgers eat earthworms, insects, and mice.

PREDATORS
Tawny owls, foxes, and other top predators live on small mammals and birds.

DECOMPOSERS
Funguses, earthworms, and bacteria break down fallen leaves. Wood-eaters like bracket fungi and beetles rot branches and dead trees.

Badgers build burrows, known as "setts," by tunneling under the forest floor. Their short legs are ideal for scurrying through narrow spaces. Badgers mainly hunt at night—they have weak eyesight, but an extremely good sense of smell.

Because trees are bare in winter, there is a brief period in spring when sunlight can reach the forest floor and the temperature is warm enough for plants—like bluebells, violets, and primroses—to carpet the ground.

UNDERGROUND WEBS
The litter is laced with networks of microscopic fibers like underground webs. These are the bodies of woodland fungi—each one is called a mycelium. Fungi, which digest living or dead plant matter, are vital for breaking down leaf litter. When two mycelia meet underground, they grow fruiting bodies, which we call mushrooms. These produce thousands of tiny spores that grow into the next generation of fungi.

HARVESTING FENCES
Beneath the tallest branches are small trees like dogwood and hazel. In Europe, these were once cut down every few years ("coppiced") to make tool handles or fence posts.

WHERE DID I PUT THAT?
In the fall, squirrels, chipmunks, and jays gather large seeds like acorns, chestnuts, and hazlenuts, and store them in the ground. If seeds are never collected, they grow into new trees.

THE BIG SLEEP
Like this hedgehog, many mammals hibernate (go into a deep sleep) to survive the winter. Their temperature drops, their breathing slows, and they are hard to wake.

fallen forests

Deciduous forests have been more **affected** by human activity than *any other biome*, since they grow in the areas of fertile soil and relatively gentle climate that are most popular for humans to live in. Huge areas, especially in **China** and **Europe**, were *cut down* long ago to make way for cultivation. Most existing deciduous forest is *regrown* (so it's called "secondary forest"), and only tiny *fragments* of original **forest** remain.

Creatures in a broken-up forest can't

The spectacular Reeve's pheasant measures about 6 ft 6 in (2 m) from beak to tail.

Vulnerable pheasants Over the centuries, large areas of China have been cleared for rice fields. Since the 1950s, forests have been cut down to fuel China's new industries. Now, native birds like the Reeve's pheasant are under serious threat.

On the edge Breaking up a forest into patches creates a larger area of "edge" than exists in one large forest, and results in much less "middle" or deep forest. So plants and animals that prefer the edge, like shrubs and rodents (including the yellow-necked mouse, above) thrive, and those that like deep forest suffer.

Fruits of the oak tree, acorns (below) contain a single seed, which is particularly rich in nutrients.

Beech nut case

Acorn

Sweet chestnut

Sycamore

To travel as far from the parent tree as possible, sycamore seeds (above) whirl away on "wings."

Horse chestnuts look like ordinary chestnuts, but people can't eat them.

Horse chestnut

Seed bounty Every few years, deciduous trees produce far more seeds than usual. These are called mast years. During mast years, there are too many seeds for animals like mice and birds to eat, so lots of seeds survive and grow into new trees. But because this seed glut doesn't happen every year, the population of seed-eating birds and mice doesn't increase. Scientists don't really know what triggers mast years, but in some plants they are related to very high temperatures the year before. As temperatures rise because of climate change, mast years may happen more often. If they do, seed eaters could increase in number and eat more seeds, leaving very few to grow into new trees.

Gray squirrel

easily adapt to change.

Leafy corridors Small patches of forest are like islands in a sea of open land, and this makes it hard for forest species to change their location in response to climate change. One solution is to link the patches with narrow strips of specially planted forest that animals can move through.

On the move To keep pace with climate change, woodland plants and animals will have to migrate toward the poles. Experts think the right climate for temperate forests will move about 3,300 ft (1,000 m) a year. But plants and animals, such as the southern flying squirrel, can't keep up.

Dry and drier With climate change, summer heat waves and droughts may increase, making trees dry and parched. The European beech tree, which has shallow roots, will struggle to survive in dry summers, and may disappear altogether from the southern edge of its range.

coming together

When great-tit chicks hatch in spring, their parents need a good supply of small caterpillars to feed them. In European woodlands, they rely on the winter moth, whose caterpillars eat oak leaves. Once the caterpillars start eating, there is a huge abundance of them, but this period lasts only a few weeks, and it happens more quickly if the weather is warmer. Songbirds such as great tits need to time their egg laying so they have hungry mouths to feed just when there are lots of caterpillars. With climate change, spring temperatures have been increasing for the past 25 years in Northern Europe, and oak buds are opening about 10 days earlier. But it's not easy for the moth and the great tit to change their timing to match. In some places, young great tits are missing out on the feast because their mother does not lay her eggs early enough.

Feed the birds in your yard to help them survive while they are adjusting to climate change.

Adult winter moths mate and lay eggs in winter, and the eggs should hatch just as the new oak leaves start to grow.

If the caterpillars hatch too early, they will starve. If they hatch too late, the oak leaves will be too old, too tough, and too full of bitter tannin to eat.

As spring gets earlier, great tits are at risk because they are not laying their eggs in time to catch the earlier caterpillar glut.

logging

THE GOOD, THE BAD, AND THE CRIMINAL

People need wood—in theory, wood is a sustainable resource that we *should* use for buildings and fuel. In well-managed forests, a tree is planted for every tree that's cut down so the total amount of forest doesn't change. But because there are more and more people on the Earth all the time, more and more wood is being used. (During the last 40 years, global lumber use has more than doubled, and paper use in particular has more than *tripled*.) In tropical countries, the total amount of forest cover on the land has dropped from 53 percent in 1985 to 46 percent in 2005. Much of the forest that's left is being damaged by logging activities, or replaced by plantations of tree crops. Over the same period, forest cover in the temperate regions of Asia, Europe, and North America has risen from 22 percent to 27 percent because more forest is being planted than cleared in these areas. About three percent of the world's forests have been planted just to produce wood, but these unnatural forests don't provide homes for local wildlife the way natural forests do.

Reduce paper consumption by cleaning up kitchen spills with a cloth instead of a paper towel.

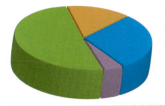

OF THE WORLD'S WOOD HARVEST:

- 51% is burned for fuel
- 29% is cut into planks and veneers
- 15% is pulped for paper, or chipped
- 5% is used for other things, such as telephone poles

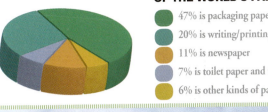

OF THE WORLD'S PAPER:

- 47% is packaging paper/card
- 20% is writing/printing paper
- 11% is newspaper
- 7% is toilet paper and tissues
- 6% is other kinds of paper

Stolen forests Illegal logging is a serious international problem—half the lumber cut in the Russian far east, for example, is taken without permission, while in Indonesia, up to 80 percent of lumber is illegal. We don't know what effect this has on wildlife, but it certainly effects the economies of the countries involved, since they can't collect tax on this industry.

mediterranean

In Australia, this scrubland is called the Mallee. Here, there are lots of eucalyptus plants and a few kangaroos.

On the western edge of each continental land mass, there are places where winters are wet, but summers are hot and dry. Here, where the average temperature is 77°F (25°C), and it often reaches 95°F (35°C), there is a special biome. There are five of these, but the biggest is near the Mediterranean Sea, which gives the biome its name. Because so many people live there, lots of woodland is already lost—trees have been cut or burned, and the land is grazed by livestock. What's left is mostly scrub, with evergreen shrubs instead of trees.

Climate change will turn up the heat and make summers even drier in these regions. Fire will be more frequent, and crops that need to be watered, like citrus fruits, may be hard to grow.

The bright yellow Cleopatra butterfly is a common sight in spring and early summer.

Native to southern Europe, rabbits like dry, open scrublands. They were introduced artificially to other countries (like Chile and Australia), where they cause trouble by thriving at the expense of native animals.

HOME OF HERBS

Lavender

Herbs like thyme, lavender, and rosemary make their home in the Mediterranean scrub ecosystem. Their small, waxy leaves conserve water, and their scented oils protect the leaves from fungi and grazing animals.

CONCRETE COAST

Each summer, 220 million tourists vacation in the Med. As well as damaging sea life, these people use up precious freshwater—swimming pools and golf courses alone need millions of gallons every day.

BAD BLUE GUM

Australian blue gum trees have been planted in the Mediterranean for wood and paper. The plantations don't support much wildlife, and the trees suck up water from deep underground and leave the soil dry.

scrub ecosystem

Wild goat

Bighorn sheep

Agile beasts Wild goats, sheep, and other climbers who live here look for food over large areas. Predators like lynx, hawks, and eagles feed on small mammals. There are many reptiles and insects in the scrub.

Protea flower

Hummingbird

Spanish imperial eagle

Gryfon vulture

PROTEA
With heads up to 1 ft (30 cm) across, proteas thrive in the poor scrub soil.

HUMMINGBIRD
Native to the Americas, tiny hummingbirds feed on flowers and insects.

EAGLE
An endangered species, the Spanish imperial eagle eats small birds and mammals.

VULTURE
A large, fierce, bird of prey, the gryfon vulture (also griffin, griffon, or gryphon) mate for life.

BIGHORN SHEEP
Bighorn sheep graze on grasses and shrubs, and absorb minerals by licking salty stones.

WILD GOAT
Another creature that feeds on grass, the wild goat has small hooves with special nonslip ridges.

To cope with dry summers, this aleppo pine has needles or waxy leaves that hold moisture. Most trees are evergreen, so they make use of any growing time during the wet winters.

In southern Europe and north Africa, the scrubland is called the Maquis (this is the Mediterranean island of Panarea); in California, it's the Chaparral; and in Chile, it's the Matorral.

ROMAN RICHES
The Mediterranean region was the seat of the Roman Empire, which ruled Europe for 500 years from the first century BCE. Its riches were partly built on the oil from olive trees native to this area.

CLEVER CORK
The traditional management of cork-oak forest is the best example of low-impact, sustainable forestry in the world, since trees are never cut down. The cork bark is stripped off every ten years, but it always grows back.

Cork bark, bottle stops, tile

LOVE TO BURN
Fire, fanned by strong, dry winds, often burns vegetation in summer. Some trees, like eucalyptus and scrub oak, quickly regrow from underground roots. Others, like pines or Australian Banksia shrubs, need the heat from fire to release their seeds from cones or woody fruits. Flowers like the fire lilies of southern Africa (right) wait underground for the heat or ash from fires to trigger their growth. The year after a fire, orchids flower profusely in the blackened earth.

the giant panda

CHINA'S GIANT PANDA, ONE OF THE RAREST BEARS IN THE WORLD, IS A WORLDWIDE SYMBOL OF CONSERVATION

Giant pandas live in mountain forests in western China, near Tibet. They like these forests because their very favorite food grows there—bamboo. (Pandas are different from most other bears, which eat meat.) Bamboo growth is incredibly lush in these mountain forests, which is a good thing because pandas eat vast amounts. There isn't much energy in a bamboo shoot, so the bears have to consume at least 18 lb (8 kg) of them every day—in fact, they don't really have time to do anything else. One of the reasons panda numbers are so depleted (there are only a few thousand left) is that each area of bamboo dies spontaneously every 40–60 years. Unfortunately, many of the mountain forests have been cleared, so there are few areas of bamboo left. Lots of pandas die when the bamboo in their small patch disappears.

China

In addition to keeping pandas in special reserves, scientists are monitoring them in the wild, mapping their habitats, and trying to understand their mating habits in order to help them breed more easily.

Although grown pandas are large bears, their babies are incredibly tiny. They're about the length of a pencil when they're born, and pink all over with a small amount of white fur.

No place to go The destruction of China's forests (traditionally to plant rice fields, and recently to provide fuel for industry) has reduced the panda population dramatically. In recent years, however, the Chinese government has taken major steps to preserve them—they have protected the forests from logging, passed laws against poaching or smuggling panda skins, and organized special reserves where pandas can live and breed in safety.

MAKING A DIFFERENCE

Temperate forests are awesome places.

They can be terrifying and creepy, like the Forbidden Forest near Harry Potter's school or the woods where Hansel and Gretel were lost. Or they can be safe sanctuaries, like Robin Hood's Sherwood Forest or Lothlorien, where the Galadrim elves live in *Lord of the Rings.* However they are seen, temperate forests are precious. When we cut down trees, we should do it wisely so the forests can thrive along with all the creatures that use them.

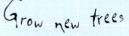

Grow new trees

Don't throw it away

When you've finished with paper, recycle it. Paper can be recycled about six times before its fibers are too broken to be strong enough. Then it can be mixed with new wood pulp to strengthen it. Buy recycled paper products whenever you can.

what you can do

Always tuck a clean cotton handkerchief into your pocket or purse—tissues waste a huge amount of paper.

FSC © Look for the Forest Stewardship Council logo on books, paper, furniture, shelving, and lumber. There are over 222,400,000 acres (90,000,000 hectares) of FSC-certified forests around the world, and several thousand different products are made from their wood.

www.fsc.org

Children who care about trees will look after them when they grow up.

"He that plants trees loves others beside himself."

Thomas Fuller, English writer, 1732

KNOW THE DEBATE

what's being done

• **The Forest Stewardship Council (FSC)** was set up to guarantee that every forest its wood comes from, and the people who live in or near each forest, are well looked after.

• **Lots of different countries** are passing laws to protect their precious forests from logging, clearing, mining, and similar exploitation.

• **National networks** are gathering people's information and observations about nature so they can monitor the effects of climate change. This will only work if lots of people record things like when a particular butterfly appeared in spring, when the first swallow arrived, and how often the grass needs cutting.

what we can do

• **Plant trees** and look after them for a long time to help control climate change. Trees absorb carbon dioxide and store the harmful carbon in their wood.

• **Look for a charity** that will help you to sponsor a tree in a protected forest—or give one as a present!

• **Support the natural cork industry.** Encourage wine producers to seal bottles with cork stoppers rather than metal or plastic caps.

• **Spend time in your nearest wood.** Walk in it, smell it, and find its secrets. Watch the seasons change, and above all, enjoy it.

If you go into a forest for a walk or a picnic, don't drop litter or leave a fire smouldering—forest fires destroy trees and cause pollution.

Use less paper

Never throw away a piece of paper that has not been covered on both sides. Open envelopes carefully, so you can use them more than once. Find information on the internet instead of buying magazines, and look for paper made from other fibers, like hemp or straw. Reuse greeting cards by cutting off the front to make postcards or gift tags. And, of course, RECYCLE!

what you can do
Buy or build a birdhouse in your yard to provide protection and shelter for local species.

DESERTS

The Sun beats down on a camel train as it crosses a *vast expanse* of sand dunes in a hot, dry, shadeless desert.

DESERTS

But is the desert as empty as it appears? Insects scuttle around on the sand; plant seeds lie dormant below the surface; and many animals from rodents to reptiles seek shelter in underground burrows, waiting to come out in the cool night air to hunt for food.

where on earth...?

Deserts are arid areas of land that receive less than 10 in (25 cm) of rain a year. Deserts currently cover about one-fifth of the Earth's land surface. They can be found in all kinds of locations, from mountains to coasts—and even Antarctica.

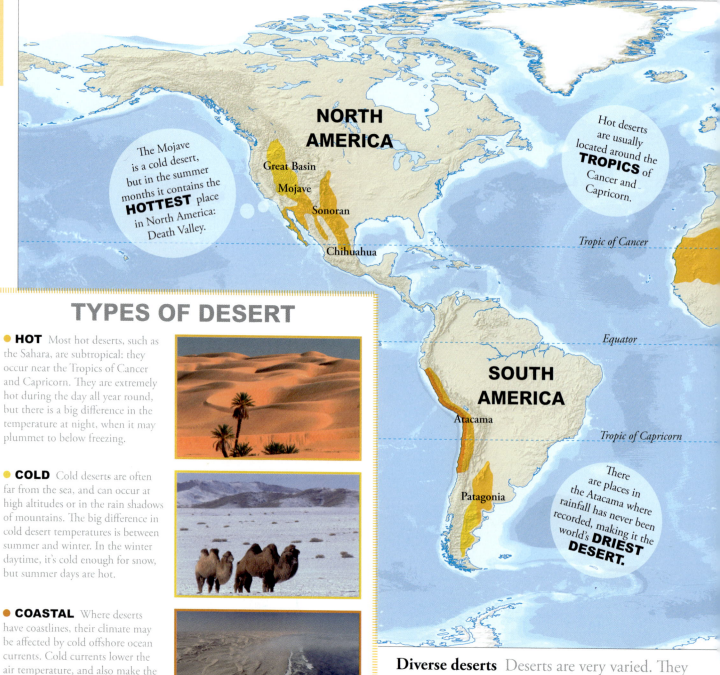

NORTH AMERICA

The Mojave is a cold desert, but in the summer months it contains the **HOTTEST** place in North America: Death Valley.

Great Basin

Mojave

Sonoran

Chihuahua

Hot deserts are usually located around the **TROPICS** of Cancer and Capricorn.

Tropic of Cancer

Equator

SOUTH AMERICA

Atacama

Tropic of Capricorn

Patagonia

There are places in the Atacama where rainfall has never been recorded, making it the world's **DRIEST DESERT.**

TYPES OF DESERT

● **HOT** Most hot deserts, such as the Sahara, are subtropical: they occur near the Tropics of Cancer and Capricorn. They are extremely hot during the day all year round, but there is a big difference in the temperature at night, when it may plummet to below freezing.

● **COLD** Cold deserts are often far from the sea, and can occur at high altitudes or in the rain shadows of mountains. The big difference in cold desert temperatures is between summer and winter. In the winter daytime, it's cold enough for snow, but summer days are hot.

● **COASTAL** Where deserts have coastlines, their climate may be affected by cold offshore ocean currents. Cold currents lower the air temperature, and also make the air even more dry. Not every desert on the coast is affected because not every coast has a cold current.

Diverse deserts Deserts are very varied. They may be large or small, and can be found all over the world, in tropical and temperate areas and at high and low altitudes. But they do have things in common: strong sunshine,

WHAT CAUSES DESERTS?

As air moves around the Earth, it collects water through evaporation and loses it again through precipitation (rain, snow, hail, and sleet). Dry air contains little water vapor, so the land it passes over receives little rain.

TYPES OF DESERT

Deserts can be classified in various ways, such as by temperature (hot or cold), or physical characteristics (sandy or rocky). In this book deserts are described as hot or cold. Both types may be affected by ocean currents, turning parts of them into coastal deserts.

DESERT MARGINS

A desert is a place with little rain, but toward the edge of a desert, more rain falls. This means more plants can grow, and the land turns from a desert into grassland. Most desert people live in these semiarid areas between a desert and a grassland.

PROTECTING THE DESERT

You might think that climate change can't affect deserts, which are already hot and dry—but it may make them hotter and drier. Water would become even scarcer and so plants would die off, leaving no food for animals.

DESERTIFICATION

An even bigger problem than climate change is that of desertification—the spread of desert conditions into other biomes. Nearly three-quarters of the world's drylands (grassland and dry forest) are at risk of turning into desert.

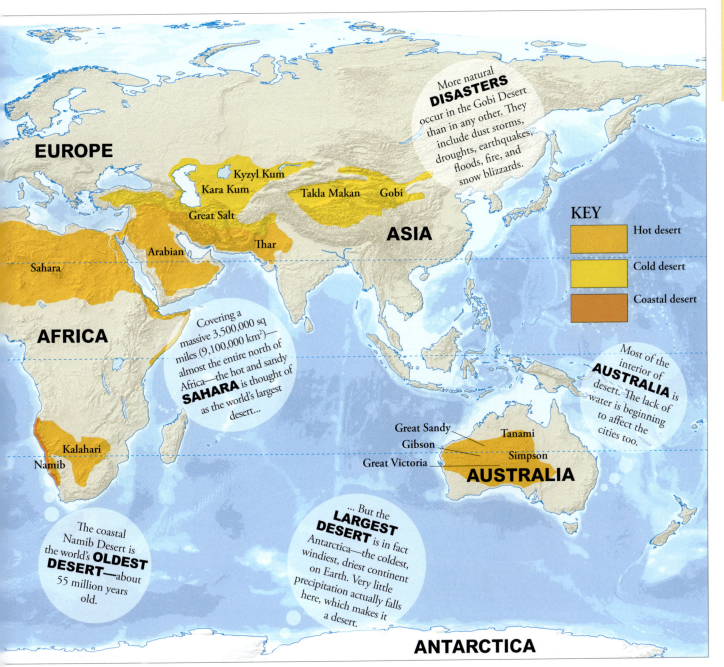

EUROPE

More natural **DISASTERS** occur in the Gobi Desert than in any other. They include dust storms, droughts, earthquakes, floods, fire, and snow blizzards.

Kyzyl Kum
Kara Kum
Great Salt
Takla Makan   Gobi
Thar
Arabian
ASIA

Sahara

KEY

Hot desert
Cold desert
Coastal desert

AFRICA

Covering a massive 3,500,000 sq miles (9,100,000 km²) almost the entire north of Africa—the hot and sandy **SAHARA** is thought of as the world's largest desert...

Most of the interior of **AUSTRALIA** is desert. The lack of water is beginning to affect the cities too.

Kalahari
Namib

Great Sandy
Gibson   Tanami
Great Victoria   Simpson
AUSTRALIA

The coastal Namib Desert is the world's **OLDEST DESERT**—about 55 million years old.

... But the **LARGEST DESERT** is in fact Antarctica—the coldest, windiest, driest continent on Earth. Very little precipitation actually falls here, which makes it a desert.

ANTARCTICA

harsh winds——and, of course, dryness. There are occasional, sudden downpours, but most of the time rainfall is so low that not many plants can grow, which means there is little food for animals. Plants also provide ground cover. Without them, soil can blow away, leaving just sand and rock. This bare ground reflects heat from the Sun, warming the air. Warm air holds in more water than cold air, so now there's even less chance of rain falling in the desert.

desert basics

TROPICAL RAIN FORESTS
get more than 70 in (180 cm) of rain per year, which is why they have such lush vegetation.

TEMPERATE FORESTS
get 20-80 in (50-200 cm) of rain per year.

GRASSLANDS
get **10-30 in** (25-75 cm) of rain per year. It is enough to support grass, but not many trees.

DESERTS usually get less than **10 in** (25 cm) of rain per year, which is not enough for most plants to grow.

There are four things that all *deserts* have in common: **lack of rainfall**, strong **sunshine**, and **wind**, which all together make a **sparse landscape**. All animals and plants that live in deserts have *adapted* to survive the harsh environment.

A thorny devil makes the most of the little water found in Australian deserts by drinking dew that collects in its spines.

How much rain? Rainfall is one of the factors that makes an area a particular biome. A desert is a desert because it gets very little rain, so not many plants can grow there. Where more rain falls, more plants grow, making grassland. Where lots of rain falls, enough trees can grow to create forests.

Wind shapes the landscape, causing

The power of the wind One of the effects of having little vegetation in the desert is that there are few large trees to break up the wind. Strong gusts often pick up sand and dust, forming dust storms that blast against rocks, grinding them down and creating more sand.

Strong sunshine

Stand in the middle of a desert, look up at the sky, and it's easy to see why deserts are hot: there are no clouds to block out the sunshine. It's the same reason why deserts are cold at night—there are no clouds to keep in the heat.

JUST ADD WATER!

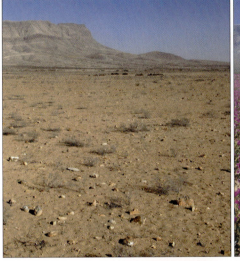

Springing into action

Most of the time, there are few plants to be seen in the desert because of the lack of rain. But when it falls, there can be a brief, beautiful blooming. Seeds lie dormant under the sand, waiting perhaps years for the unpredictable rain. Then they quickly germinate, bloom, and create new seeds for the next generation of plants—all within a few weeks.

mountains to crumble.

It has taken millions of years for ice, water, and wind to wear down the mountains into tiny grains of sand and dust.

hot desert ecosystem

The Sahara Desert, in Africa, is the world's largest hot desert. Seemingly empty but for sand and rocks, the land actually supports a variety of wildlife—but it's a battle to survive in such an extreme environment. There are few plants to give shade, and winds can be strong. The clear blue sky has no clouds for rain or to protect against the Sun, so daytime temperatures are very high. The lack of cloud cover also lets the heat escape at night, so the hot desert turns very cold when the Sun goes down.

Average Saharan temperatures
Daytime: 136°F (58°C)
Nighttime: 14°F (-10°C)

The Sahara is about the same size as mainland Europe or the US.

Most lizards eat both plants and invertebrates such as insects, but the dabb lizard is herbivorous—it eats only plants.

Vultures and other birds take advantage of the warm air thermals that rise above the desert, allowing the birds to glide.

Survival skills It's hard to find food and water in the desert. The resources are scarce, and the extreme heat and lack of shade makes searching difficult. Desert animals are adapted to this type of existence; for example, some get all their water from their food. They also have ways of keeping cool, such as spending the day in cool burrows, coming out at night to hunt.

WATER IN THE DESERT
The lushest scenery in the desert is at an oasis. These pools form where underground water comes to the surface. Oases are a shady haven for animals, which come to fill up on leafy food as well as water.

Desert food chain Life in the desert relies on vegetation. Even carnivorous animals that do not eat plants, eat animals that do. But there are not many plants in the desert to support the chain, so the animals here are generally smaller and fewer in number than in other ecosystems.

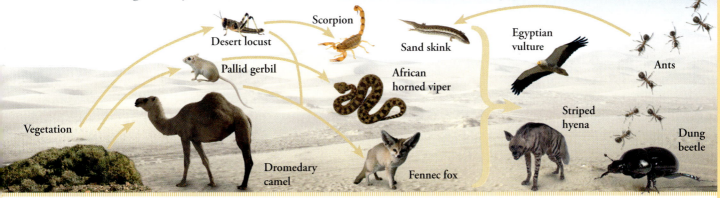

Desert locust
Scorpion
Sand skink
Egyptian vulture
Pallid gerbil
African horned viper
Ants
Vegetation
Striped hyena
Dromedary camel
Fennec fox
Dung beetle

PRODUCERS
Plants need three things to grow: sunshine, nutrients from the ground, and water. Sunshine and nutrients are plentiful, but water is often in short supply.

PRIMARY CONSUMERS
While the majority of plant eaters are invertebrates such as insects, there are some small and large mammals that are herbivorous too.

SECONDARY CONSUMERS
Being quite small animals, desert carnivores aim for small prey. They would not kill a full-grown camel, although a baby may be targeted. The predators may eat other meat eaters as well as herbivores.

SCAVENGERS & DECOMPOSERS
Scavengers such as vultures and hyenas aid decomposition by breaking up and eating dead animals. Ants take bits of carcass underground, where "leftovers" act as fertilizer. Dung beetles do the same thing with feces, to the same effect. Any other waste is broken down by bacteria.

Camels can stock up on food and turn it into fat, which they store in their humps. They can live off this fat for weeks without needing to eat or drink.

Gerbils spend the day in their burrows, which are cooler and more humid than the desert outside. They emerge at night when it is cooler to hunt for food.

The Sahara is mostly made up of rocks and gravel, but there is still more than enough sand to form massive dunes.

THE BURROWERS
The jerboa is an expert recycler. Sealing itself in an underground den away from the heat, it is able to recapture the moisture from its breath, so it rarely needs to drink.

TWICE AS USEFUL
Hunting in the dark, the Fennec fox uses its large ears like satellite dishes to pinpoint the position of its prey. The ears' large surface area also loses heat, helping to keep the fox cool.

FILLING UP
Camels can go without water for up to two weeks. When thirsty, they can drink up to 32 gallons (120 liters)—a volume that would be fatal to most animals.

WARMING UP
The desert heat has its advantages. Reptiles are cold-blooded: they warm up and cool down depending on the environment. They need the sunshine to warm up and get active.

desert destruction

Deserts have always been subject to *natural* change, growing or shrinking with changes in rainfall. Millions of years ago, North Africa was covered by a sea; today it is home to the world's biggest hot desert. The main threat to deserts is not nature, but people. **Human activity** is having an enormous effect on desert wildlife, as well as the landscape. Plants and animals that have evolved to survive in the desert cannot cope with the rapid changes brought about by people, and so they die out.

This fossil of a sea creature was found in the Sahara Desert, proving that the now arid area was once under water.

Arid areas are thought of as untouched,

Climate change Already hot and dry, deserts are under threat of becoming hotter and drier due to climate change. Without water, no plants can grow. Without plants, the whole food chain collapses. Once the plants and animals disappear, there is little hope of the desert recovering.

Overgrazing The introduction of nonnative species into deserts has been devastating. Brought in by farmers who need the meat, milk, wool, and leather, domestic animals such as goats compete with wild animals for food. They also strip the plants bare, which can kill the plant, leaving the ground open to wind erosion.

Building Whether it's a tourist resort or a town, building settlements in the desert puts a strain on resources. Nomads move from place to place, so when water and pasture for animals run low, they move on and the stocks can recover. But when people stay in one place, there is no chance for the land to replenish itself.

In the center of each circle is a pipe that revolves and sprinkles water over the plants. Crops may include tomatoes and cucumbers, which need a lot of water.

Going green isn't always good The most limiting factor in a desert is the lack of water. Farmers trying to make a living use irrigation—but these huge green crop fields might do more harm than good, as the water being piped in drains underground resources and empties lakes vast distances away. The crops themselves also suck the goodness from the soil, making it infertile.

but people are changing the landscape.

Overhunting The main threat to the balance of wildlife in the desert is overhunting, which is done for meat, fur, or even sport. The oryx is under threat of extinction, but, like every species, they have a place in the ecosystem. The food chain and the environment will suffer if any part of it is missing.

Mining Below the surface of most deserts lie rich deposits of minerals, from oil to diamonds and gold. In the past, it was hard to access the minerals in deserts, but modern technology has overcome this. However, in doing so, the land is being ripped up, killing off the plants that provide food for animals.

Dune riding Hurtling over dunes in a quad bike or jeep looks like fun, but it actually destroys the dunes. It can cause the sand to slip, and also kills animals that hide below the sand's surface.

Be an ecotourist! If you visit a desert, stay in a resort that cares for the environment— and avoid dune buggies.

the saguaro cactus

PROTECTING A NATIONAL TREASURE OF NORTH AMERICA—AND THE ANIMALS THAT DEPEND ON IT FOR FOOD AND SHELTER

That most iconic of desert plants, the saguaro cactus, is an endangered species. It is found only in one area, and it grows *very* slowly—if one gets damaged, it might never recover. In 1933, the Saguaro National Park was set up to protect the plant from habitat-destroying fires, vandals, and collectors who harvested the cactus for sale. Yet the saguaro was nearly lost from there, too, due to severe winters and livestock grazing: as cattle fed in the shade of other desert trees they trampled on young cactuses growing in the shadows. Now cattle have been excluded from the park, the saguaro can stand tall once more.

Avoid picking plants that grow in the desert—you might endanger the species, as well as the animals that need it.

Sonoran Desert

Giant saguaro cacti grow in the Sonoran Desert, North America. All true cacti are native to this continent.

Some species of bats and birds rely on the saguaro's nectar and fruit for food. Gila woodpeckers even live in the plant, carving nest holes into the stem.

A saguaro can live for more than 200 years. It can reach a magnificent 50 ft (15 m) tall, despite growing less than 1 in (2.5 cm) per year.

MOVING ON People used to think nothing of ripping up saguaros if they got in the way. But times change—now cacti are carefully moved to a new home before roads are built through where they once stood.

cold desert ecosystem

Cold deserts share many features with hot deserts, such as strong winds and a sparse landscape. But they have one major difference: they freeze in the winter. Many cold deserts are actually drier than hot ones, because most of the precipitation falls as snow rather than rain, which animals cannot drink. It also covers the vegetation, making food hard to find. The best time of year is spring, when melting snow provides a little water for plants and animals. Come the summer, the hot Sun dries the land once more.

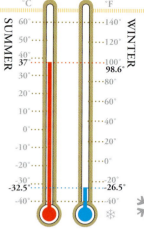

SUMMER   WINTER
37   98.6°
-32.5°   -26.5°

Average Gobi temperatures
Summer: 98.6°F (37°C)
Winter: -26.5°F (-32.5°C)

Thick wool keeps the Bactrian camel warm in the winter. Molting starts in the spring, leaving a light covering for summer.

There are two main groups of nomads living in the Gobi: Khalka Mongols and Kazakhs. Their sturdy tents, called gers, are thickly padded to keep out the cold, yet are easy to take down and transport.

Life in the Gobi Desert In a cold desert, low winter temperatures are more of a problem than heat for plants and animals, and it is made even colder by windchill. It can be difficult for animals to find enough to eat, so to avoid this shortage some animals store fat, while others hibernate.

Traditional desert life

The Khalka Mongols that live in the Gobi are pastoralists—they keep livestock, living off the meat, milk, and wool that the animals provide. They live in tune with the desert, moving to new pasture up to 10 times a year, which gives the vegetation time to recover.

Gifts of the Gobi Despite its stark appearance, the desert has useful resources both above and below ground. Some are taken in order to make huge profits, whereas others are needed simply to survive.

Wind turbine

Gold

Coal

Domesticated
Bactrian camel

Fossilized
skull of a
Protoceratops

PRECIOUS METALS
Many deserts have valuable minerals below their surface. The Gobi has rich deposits of gold and copper, which are mined by companies from all over the world.

COAL AND OIL
Fossil fuels such as coal and oil are major sources of energy. Improved transportation has made it easy for the fuels to be taken into China and across east Asia.

WIND POWER
Strong Gobi winds are ideal for wind turbines, which generate electricity as they turn. It is a good alternative to fossil fuels as wind can't run out, but coal will.

ANIMALS
Bactrian camels have been domesticated for use as beasts of burden, as well as for their wool, meat, and milk. Nomads also keep horses, cattle, sheep, and goats.

DINOSAUR FOSSILS
Fossilized bones, eggs, and nests have all been found in the Gobi. They were the first finds to provide evidence of dinosaur behavior.

Golden eagles feed on marmots and small foxes, which they catch in their sharp talons as they swoop down onto their prey.

Unlike rodents in hot deserts, which burrow to keep from overheating, gerbils in the Gobi burrow to keep warm.

SUPER SHRUBS
There are even fewer plants in cold deserts than in hot ones. The saxaul tree can grow in the Gobi because it loses little water through its small leaves. It also stores water in its bark.

BIRDS OF PREY
Kazakh nomads train female golden eagles to hunt for animals and bring them back for food or for their skins. The birds are flown hungry to encourage them to hunt.

LIVING LARDERS
Like the camel, a leopard gecko can store food in its body. When it finds vegetation, it eats more than it needs and converts the rest to fat, which it stores in its tail for when food is short.

HIBERNATION
In winter, food is scarce and the climate cold. Bobak marmots avoid both by hibernating and living off their fat reserves. They hibernate in family groups for up to half a year.

the bactrian camel

It's a challenge to catch a glimpse of a wild Bactrian camel. One of the world's rarest mammal species, there are fewer than 950 left in the world today—and those that exist are very timid. For centuries they have been hunted for their meat and hide, so it's understandable that they flee from people. They also avoid other animals, but this makes it hard for them to find food and water, especially in a desert where people are settling near oases. But perhaps the biggest modern threat to the wild Bactrian is habitat destruction. Road building, nuclear testing, and illegal mining have all changed the face of the Gobi. There are breeding programs to help save the endangered species, but can it survive if the land itself is under threat?

At one time, Bactrians roamed central Asia. Now they are confined to three small pockets of the Takla Makan and Gobi deserts.

Wild Bactrians will not come to this oasis: domestic animals (including camels) and people scare them. The livestock also eats most of the plants in the desert, leaving none for the Bactrian.

Las Vegas **desert city**

IS THE DESERT A GOOD PLACE TO BUILD NEW HOMES FOR A GROWING POPULATION? OR HAS LAS VEGAS GONE TOO FAR?

1905
POPULATION
0

2005
POPULATION
1,796,380

1930

1990

FROM SMALL BEGINNINGS...

People first went to Las Vegas for its freshwater spring—an oasis in the desert. The town grew to become a railroad stop, and by 1930, 5,000 people were living there. To meet the water needs of the population, the Hoover Dam was completed in 1935, creating Lake Mead as a reservoir.

... TO SPRAWLING CITIES

Since the end of World War II, when there was a boom in tourism and gambling, the city has not stopped growing. In 1990 nearly a million people were living in Clark County, a number that has almost doubled again today. There is simply not enough water in Lake Mead for them all.

The need for fresh water in Las Vegas, the US's fastest

Las Vegas lies in the Mojave Desert. The city, in Nevada, is part of a larger urban area called Clark County.

Construction site? A desert might seem like an ideal empty site for a city, but animals and plants are put under threat as their sources of shelter, food, and water are lost. Transportation links also carve up the desert, destroying even more land.

Lighting up the night sky wastes electricity. Turn off unnecessary lights when you leave a room or go to bed.

More than a DROP in the desert...

In addition to its 1.8 million residents, Las Vegas attracts 30 million tourists a year. With pools, fountains, water-based shows, and personal use, it works out that each person in the city uses 40 percent more water than the US national average. But water supplies, which are already limited in a desert, are predicted to run too low to meet demands by 2025. With hotels relying on their attractions to bring in money, this won't be an easy problem to solve.

(gallons per person per day)

Las Vegas
307
(1,165 liters)

US average
190
(720 liters)

Los Angeles
140
(530 liters)

TRANSPORTATION TENSION
Water isn't the only issue to consider when building in the desert. They have few natural resources, so Las Vegas is not able to produce much. Almost everything needed in the city, from food to clothing, is brought in by road or air, which causes pollution.

If water displays disappear from Las Vegas, will the tourists still come?

growing city, is so great, demand could soon outstrip supply.

dried up and deserted

Desertification is what happens when once-fertile land becomes *useless* and turns to desert—and it's mainly due to *human activity.* Misusing the land causes vegetation to die out, which leads to soil erosion. Seventy percent of drylands, such as grasslands and forests, are at risk of becoming desert—that's one-third of all the land on Earth, affecting 1 billion people and countless animals and plants.

Ostriches are native to South African grasslands, areas that are turning to desert. Many animals living there will die out if they have nowhere to go for food and shelter.

Wherever you live in the world, it's important not to waste water. You could turn off the faucet while you brush your teeth.

Some causes of desertification...

Overpopulation Many nomads have settled in desert margins where there is more vegetation, but there are too many people for the land to support. The soil becomes exhausted by farming, and livestock overgraze the plants. Left bare and exposed, topsoil is blown away, leaving sand and rocks—and creating desert.

Fire People in urbanized desert margins set fires on purpose as a way of controlling natural fires. They clear the land of vegetation that might burn uncontrollably, creating fire breaks to protect their property. But this kills off slow-growing native plants, and also destroys sources of food and shelter for animals.

Salinization Irrigation provides water for plants, but it can also turn the land infertile. Minerals left behind when water evaporates leave a salty crust on the ground, which stops plants from growing. Salinization also occurs where there are no plants—when soil gets blown away, minerals in the ground can come to the surface.

1963   **1973**   **2001**

Lake Chad is in the Sahel, an area south of the Sahara that is quickly turning to desert. The lake contains just 5 percent of the water it held 40 years ago.

Less in, more out
Lake Chad is a vital source of water in central Africa. People use water for their animals and crops—it is even piped into the Sahara for irrigation. But there is a limited amount of water, and it's running out. There is less rainfall in the area now, and the river that feeds the lake has been diverted for use elsewhere. The lake cannot replenish and it is shrinking fast.

... and some of the ways to prevent it.

Protect native trees Tall plants help to keep land stable by acting as windbreaks, slowing down the wind to help prevent soil erosion. Native trees survive on less water than nonnative, putting less strain on the habitat. Their roots are also important: they are very long or widespread to reach water, and this helps to bind and stabilize the soil.

Sand fences Where trees have been removed, it is possible to plant new vegetation and create a sand fence to stop the desert from creeping into, and taking over, neighboring land. In China, a massive project called "The Green Wall" has been started to try to stop the spread of the Gobi Desert into exhausted farmland.

Alternative fuel One of the first sand fences in Africa proved to be a success----until people chopped down the trees for cooking fuel. Many desert dwellers live in poverty and use whatever resources they can find. By supplying alternatives such as solar-powered ovens, both the people and the land benefit.

sand **in the** city

STRONG WINDS OVER THE GOBI DESERT BRING MISERY (AND LOTS OF DUST) TO BEIJING, CHINA

The people of Beijing are getting used to a major problem that hits their city many times a year: dust. Blown in from the Gobi Desert, the fine yellow particles fill the air, causing reduced visibility and breathing difficulties. Airports are closed, cars are damaged, and people cannot work because dust even gets inside machines and computers that are kept indoors. Such storms are a natural occurrence in deserts, but as desertification swallows up farmland on the margins of the Gobi, the storms are brought closer to the cities, appearing more frequently and traveling farther. Aside from forecasting when the storms are about to hit, there is little that anyone can do except try to prevent them from getting worse. And the only way to do this is to stop desertification.

China

North America

Pacific Ocean

Dust storms can travel enormous distances. In a desert, both sand and dust get blown around, but sand is heavy and does not get lifted far—around 2 ft (50 cm) above the ground. Dust, however, can travel for thousands of miles. Gobi dust can reach the west coast of North America, turning sunsets red and making cars dusty. It also drops into the Pacific Ocean between the continents, clogging up coral reefs. The Sahara Desert, in Africa, is to blame for dust in Europe and eastern Americas. Yet it does have one benefit: the fertile dust drops into and "feeds" the Amazon Rain forest.

MAKING A DIFFERENCE

WHAT's it got to do with ME?

So you live in a town far away from a desert. Think desertification has nothing to do with you? **Think again!**

Don't waste water Water shortages occur in many places, but it's easy to get into the habit of saving water... ✱ turn off faucets ✱ take showers, rather than baths ✱ water the garden with leftover dishwater or cold coffee ✱ use a bucket of water rather than a hose to wash a car

Start planting Stop soil erosion in arid areas by replacing trees.

✱ Plant a Tree USA is a nonprofit organization that has a special program encouraging tree planting. www.plantatreeusa.com

Got a garden?
Grow plants that are suitable for your climate.

what you can do
Are you visiting a desert area? (Don't forget this includes Las Vegas and Australia!) Be an ecotourist and limit the water you use. Do you need clean towels every day?

the search for water in dry land

Many desert dwellers live in poverty and have limited resources. For them, getting water isn't as simple as turning on a faucet. But there are ways of making access to water easier.

Johads In the Thar Desert, small dams called johads are built across streams. When rain falls, the water collects behind the dam, creating a reservoir for people to use. The water also seeps into the ground, providing enough moisture for plants to grow.

Fog catchers In the Atacama Desert, water comes not from rain but from fog. Huge nets "catch" the fog, which condenses into water. Chlorine is added, the water is boiled, and people have enough safe water to drink, wash in, and cook with.

Collecting water in the Thar Desert, India

The best way to combat desertification is to prevent it happening in the first place— wherever you live in the world.

what you can do

Plan an event to mark World Day to Combat Desertification, held every year on June 17. As well as raising awareness, you could raise funds for charity.

IYDD
International Year of Deserts and Desertification

- The year 2006 was declared International Year of Deserts and Desertification (IYDD) by the **United Nations** as part of their **Convention to Combat Desertification (UNCCD)**.

- **Sub-Saharan Africa** and **South Asia** were identified as being most at threat from desertification. Other at-risk regions include Latin America and central and eastern Europe.

- One billion people in over 100 countries are affected by desertification. Many are **poor** and are **politically weak**.

- As a result of the IYDD, **national action programs** encourage governments to work with local people to preserve the land, while still being able to earn a living.

- Countries not immediately affected by desertification offer technical and financial help through **partnership agreements**.

practical ACTION

- Desertification is not just about land, but people, too. Those who live in desert margins have a vital job in protecting the land. But they still need to make a living for themselves, and often this causes a conflict of interest.

- It's important to **educate local people** in how to use desert resources. The UN has produced **kits** for children in primary schools to learn about causes and effects of desertification. Newspapers, radio, and TV all help to spread information, too.

- What **hidden assets** are there in the area? Instead of raising nonnative animals for food, which compete with native species, people in Africa could eat ostrich meat, or kangaroos in Australia.

- With enough know-how and money, **technology** can solve many problems: instead of using trees for fuel, **wind turbines** provide energy and **solar ovens** replace wood burners. Solar-powered **desalination systems** make drinking water available.

Fog catcher, Chile

How to catch fog:
As fog condenses on the giant mesh, it runs down into a gutter below the net. Instant water!

what you can do

Water shortages can occur even in areas that are not deserts. As the number of people in the world grows, fresh water is becoming a valuable resource. Never waste it!

GRASSLANDS

The grassland biome is a gentle landscape, but it contains a variety of **complex** and *diverse* habitats.

It may not look as impressive as a mountain range or rain forest, but the largest and fastest land animals live here, supported by the most common of plants: grass. This is the habitat in which humans evolved—and in which we have had a most profound influence.

GRASSLANDS

where on earth...?

Grasslands are among the world's most productive biomes. The climate in these ecosystems falls between those of deserts and forests: they are usually hot—at least in summer—and have more rainfall than a desert, but not enough to support many trees.

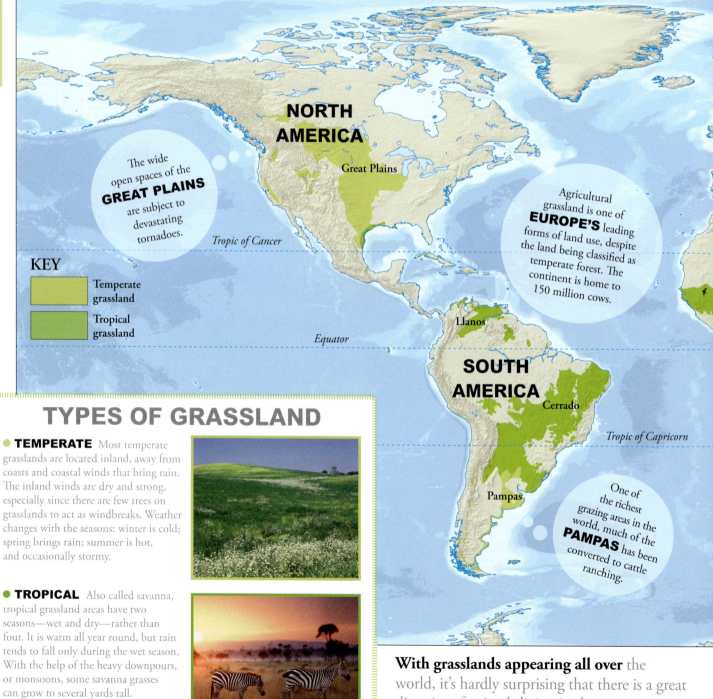

NORTH AMERICA

Great Plains

The wide open spaces of the **GREAT PLAINS** are subject to devastating tornadoes.

Tropic of Cancer

Agricultural grassland is one of **EUROPE'S** leading forms of land use, despite the land being classified as temperate forest. The continent is home to 150 million cows.

KEY

Temperate grassland

Tropical grassland

Llanos

Equator

SOUTH AMERICA

Cerrado

Tropic of Capricorn

Pampas

One of the richest grazing areas in the world, much of the **PAMPAS** has been converted to cattle ranching.

TYPES OF GRASSLAND

● **TEMPERATE** Most temperate grasslands are located inland, away from coasts and coastal winds that bring rain. The inland winds are dry and strong, especially since there are few trees on grasslands to act as windbreaks. Weather changes with the seasons: winter is cold; spring brings rain; summer is hot, and occasionally stormy.

● **TROPICAL** Also called savanna, tropical grassland areas have two seasons—wet and dry—rather than four. It is warm all year round, but rain tends to fall only during the wet season. With the help of the heavy downpours, or monsoons, some savanna grasses can grow to several yards tall.

With grasslands appearing all over the world, it's hardly surprising that there is a great diversity of animals living in these ecosystems. There is as much activity below ground as above it. Grasslands are open spaces where

GIVE AND TAKE
Grassland covers half the Earth's land surface. Much of the natural grassland has been lost to agriculture, but the total amount of grassland across the world remains the same as large areas of forest are felled to create pasture (grassland used for grazing).

GRASS OR SHRUB?
Grasslands are not just made up of grass: plenty of nonwoody, flowering plants with broad leaves—such as daisies—grow there, too. Some trees and shrubs grow on grasslands, but when there are more woody plants than grass, the land is known as shrubland.

HARD GARDENING
Many extreme natural events occur on grasslands, from monsoons, wildfires, and tornadoes to droughts and freezing temperatures. Yet far from causing problems, these events help to maintain grassland, for example, by weeding out plants that compete with the grass.

WIND POWER
In the summer, strong gusts of wind spread fires across open grassland. While fire can help grass—for example, the ash acts as fertilizer—blazes can have devastating effects. Wildlife and people can lose their homes, local sources of food, and even their lives.

WHAT ABOUT EUROPE?
This continent may be known for its rural scenery of gently rolling grassy fields and "patchwork" farms, but technically Europe is classified as temperate forest—despite much of it being cleared to create meadows or urban areas.

The **STEPPES** are so vast, they cross two continents, but are one of the least-populated areas in the world.

EUROPE

Russian steppes

Central Asian steppes

ASIA

Between the deserts and the northern coast of Australia lies the tropical **AUSTRALIAN SAVANNA.** It can be cool and dry in the winter, but summertime is hot and humid.

Indian savanna

AFRICA

Sahel

Monsoon rains help tall grasses to flourish on the **INDIAN** savanna. Tigers like to live in these grassy "forests."

Masai Mara and Serengeti

Australian savanna

AUSTRALIA

Rangeland

South African Veld

The **SERENGETI** is one of the oldest ecosystems on Earth. Its climate, vegetation, and fauna have changed little over the last million years.

ANTARCTICA

there are few places to hide from predators, so animals such as prairie dogs and voles dig burrows to shelter underground. Many nonburrowing herbivores, such as antelope, rely on speed to outrun carnivores. The grasses that form the basis of the herbivores' diets are varied, too. Cows munch on short meadow grasses, but bison on the Great Plains prefer beardgrass, which grows to 10 ft (3 m) tall. Even this is small compared to another type of grass, a variety of bamboo that reaches 115 ft (35 m)!

prairie ecosystem

Temperate grasslands such as prairies occur in every continent except Antarctica. The Great Plains of North America are vast prairies covering around 1.1 million sq miles (3 million sq km). Here, enough rain falls to support grasses, but not trees. With nothing to interrupt air flow, the prairie is a windy place. It also has long, hot summers and cold winters. Many rodents and herbivores live on the Great Plains, and these animals are essential for maintaining the grassland ecosystem.

Temperate grasslands are subject to great variations in the weather as seasons change throughout the year. Summer's scorching heat is far removed from the cold winter snow.

Soaring high over its territory, a golden eagle hunts by sight, swooping down at speed to pick up small mammals such as rodents and rabbits in its talons.

The tall and the short of it Because the Great Plains are so vast, the amount of rainfall they receive varies from place to place, and this difference shows in the vegetation. On the rainier eastern side are the tall grass prairies, where bluegrass stems can reach over 6 ft (2 m) tall. In the drier west are short grass prairies, where bunch grass reaches 12–18 in (30–45 cm).

Same difference Temperate grasslands have different names and support very different plants and animals. In South America, they are called pampas; in South Africa, veld; and in southeast Australia, rangeland. Europe's extensive downs, meadows, and pastures were created hundreds of years ago by clearing temperate forest.

GREAT GRASSES

Just as there are different temperate grasslands, there are many varieties of grass, too. Clumps of pampas grass, from South America, may reach 10 ft (3 m) tall. It can also survive fire.

Short grass prairie food chain Both short grass and tall grass ecosystems are based on the vast amount of plant matter that is eaten by herbivores. Plants that are not eaten decompose when they die, which puts nutrients back into the soil.

Black-eyed Susan

Buffalo grass

Jack rabbit

Bison

Racer snake

Black-footed ferret

Coyote

Burrowing owl

Maggots

Black tiger beetle

PRODUCERS
Grasses, with their small, green, wind-pollinated flowers, dominate the landscape. Other plants have bright flowers to attract insects.

PRIMARY CONSUMERS
Herbivores (plant-eaters) are the leading animals on the prairie. They also help to maintain it.

SECONDARY CONSUMERS
The prairie carnivores feed on invertebrates such as crickets and smaller vertebrates, including jack rabbits. Wolves and other pack animals hunt together to tackle larger prey like deer. Coyotes will also eat carrion, so they scavenge for carcasses as well as hunt for prey.

DECOMPOSERS
All animals and plants eventually die and are broken down and eaten by organisms such as beetles and fly larvae.

The 60 million bison that once roamed the Plains were hunted to near-extinction in the late 1800s. They are now being reintroduced in many areas.

Ideally suited to open country, grasses are able to survive fire, grazing, and large seasonal changes in temperature.

FLOWER POWER
Grasslands are so-called because the dominant plants are grasses. However, there are plenty of wild flowers growing on the prairie too, such as this purple coneflower.

PRAIRIE PLANT-EATERS
Mule deer are herbivores. They have broad, flat teeth for chewing plants, strong digestive systems to process grass—and long legs for fleeing from predators on the open prairie.

KEEPING SAFE
Animals have many ways to keep from being eaten. Brightly colored butterflies are avoided by birds, which know they taste bad. Other animals may use camouflage colors.

NATURE'S GARDENERS
Burrowing animals, such as ground squirrels, are extremely important to the prairie. Their digging allows air into the soil, and also "weeds out" plants, allowing the grass to thrive.

prairies under pressure

Across the world, temperate grasslands are disappearing. As much as **90 percent** of the North American tall grass prairie has been lost, along with three-quarters of the South American pampas and one-fifth of the African veld. As people divide up the land for *farming* or to build on, it becomes impossible for large herbivores to move freely over it. These animals help to maintain the grassland, and the ecosystem **suffers** without them.

Look after your lawn—it's your very own "prairie"! Gardens are home to lots of wildlife. Keep a patch of grass long and see how many animals shelter there.

About 25% of all temperate grassland

Climate change Global warming is causing a problem for short grass prairies. Warmer nights encourage some plants to germinate early, but native grasses germinate late, by which time the weeds have taken over and can successfully compete for the resources the grass needs. As a result, grass is in decline.

Fencing off When land is divided by fencing, it affects both hunter and prey. In Australia fences designed to keep dingoes off farmland also stop them from reaching kangaroos. Without predators, the kangaroos increase in number. This puts more pressure on the land and leads to overgrazing.

Pest control Prairie dogs are pests: their burrows cause injury to cattle and horses, and they carry diseases. They have been killed in such large numbers that they now occupy only 2% of their original range, and prairie-based carnivores have lost an important food source.

The Dust Bowl The roots of grasses are vital to keeping soil stable and preventing erosion. The Dust Bowl was created between 1930 and 1939 because farmers cleared prairie land for crops. Left exposed to the wind and dried out by drought, the topsoil simply blew away. Huge dust storms swept the land, no crops could grow, and famine was rife. It was a harsh lesson to learn about land clearance, yet the practice still continues.

The Dust Bowl occurred in the southern and central Great Plains, in the states of Texas, Oklahoma, Kansas, Colorado, and New Mexico. Further droughts struck farms here in the 1950s, 1970s, and as recently as 2004.

has been lost to urban development.

Tough tumbleweed Introducing alien species to the prairies has altered the balance of plants. Tumbleweed was brought in from Russia to South Dakota in 1877. By 1900, it had taken over whole areas of the west coast, choking out the native vegetation.

Monoculture Converting temperate grassland to agriculture has destroyed the natural mosaic of vegetation, replacing it with vast amounts of cotton or wheat. The crops are harvested for sale, so no nutrients return from the plants to the soil to keep it fertile.

Urban development People today tend to live settled lives and as a result build permanent homes, along with roads, schools, stores, and power plants. Grasslands are easy to build on and have few physical features such as mountains to prevent settlements from growing and creating urban sprawl.

super grass

WHAT MAKES THE SMALL, UNASSUMING, LEAFY LAWN PLANT SUCH A SURVIVOR?

Of the thousands of grass species, including cereals, bamboo, and sugar cane, perhaps the most familiar to us are the short grasses found in fields and gardens. These grasses are so common and widespread because, in the natural course of events, they're almost indestructible. Unlike most plants, grass grows from near its base, which is close to the ground—sometimes below the surface— so if the top is mown, eaten, or even burned by wildfire, it won't kill the plant. Small, flexible leaves bounce back even after heavy hooves trample on them, and wind can gust over the leaves without causing damage, which is why grass can survive on windy, treeless plains where taller plants would be too battered by wind to remain upright. Grasses can survive many natural phenomena from grazing to periods of drought—but they often fall victim to human activity.

Domestic sheep are ruminants.

Ruminant animals chew the cud to break down the grass they eat. After quickly swallowing a lot of grass, they lie down to rest, "burp" the grass (or cud) back up, and chew it into a pulp.

Ruminants don't just take from the grass, they give back, too. As their dung is broken down by fungi, nutrients are released into the soil, which supports grass regrowth.

savanna ecosystem

About 40% of tropical land is covered by savanna. These grasslands are hot all year round, but have distinct wet and dry seasons. When rain falls, it is torrential and often accompanied by lightning, which causes many grassland fires. Annual rainfall ranges from 18 in (45 cm) in Australia to more than 50 in (1.2 m) in East Africa. The wetter savanna ecosystems have trees, making the habitat more diverse and supporting a greater variety of wildlife.

Thick black clouds are the warning sign that comes ahead of a monsoon—the heavy storms that are typical of the savanna wet season. If enough rain falls, trees will be able to grow.

Only the giraffe is tall enough to browse on the uppermost foliage and flowers of the scattered acacia trees. Their attentions give the trees their characteristic flat-topped shape.

The stunning Serengeti The most well-known tropical savanna ecosystem is also one of the oldest. The Serengeti is home to a variety of ungulates, or hoofed mammals, some of which occur in vast numbers. Gazelles, zebras, and wildebeest eat different parts of the grasses, and so do not need to compete for food.

FIRE!

Seasonal fires play a vital role in maintaining savanna. The flames burn off dead plant material, creating ash that washes down into the soil and fertilizes it. After a fire, the landscape quickly recovers. Grass grows fast, more than 1 in (2.5 cm) a day, and soon the large grazing animals that fled the flames can return to feed.

Savanna predators The big cats and dogs of the savanna are expert killing machines. Some live and hunt alone, while others work together to share the work and the reward. There are some predators that supplement hunting with scavenging too.

Leopard   Lion   Hyena   Jackal   African hunting dog

LEOPARD
A solitary hunter, the leopard keeps from losing its prey to other carnivores by carrying it up into a tree.

LION
Within a lion pride, it is the lionesses that do the hunting. After a kill, the males arrive and take control of the prey. Cubs feed last.

HYENA
The powerful jaws of the hyena make it a formidable hunter as well as a scavenger. It chases its prey to exhaustion and then moves in for the kill.

JACKAL
An opportunist that hunts or scavenges for meat, but also eats fruit and berries, the black backed jackal will eat anything it can catch.

AFRICAN HUNTING DOG
By hunting in a group, African hunting dogs can tackle much larger animals than one dog could attack alone.

The largest land animal, the adult elephant has few natural enemies. Young calves are protected by the entire herd should danger threaten.

Lions form groups called prides that number anything up to 40 members.

WEAVER BIRDS
Male weaver birds construct elaborate nests out of grass and leaves. Many nests have the entrance at the bottom as a protection from predatory snakes.

WORKING TOGETHER
Oxpeckers are tolerated by animals because they remove irritating ticks, which the birds eat. But they also feed on blood, and have been known to keep their hosts' wounds bleeding.

LIVING TOGETHER
Stinging ants live in the hollowed out thorns of the acacia tree. In return for this safe home, they will emerge and attack any animal that tries to eat the acacia's leaves.

CLEANING UP
Without dung beetles, savannas would disappear under a mountain of animal droppings. They help recycle nutrients by molding dung into balls and rolling it underground.

struggling savannas

Savannas are vital to keeping Earth's climate stable. They convert as much, if not more, *carbon dioxide* into carbohydrates as **tropical rain forests** do, but they receive far less attention. Losing grassland could eventually have the same effect on global temperatures as felling forests, yet vast tracts of tropical grassland are lost each year to agriculture and urban development.

Plants absorb carbon dioxide and turn it into carbohydrates such as glucose for food.

CO_2

There is a lot of oxygen left over, which is released back into the air.

O_2

Destroying tropical grasslands could

Drying out Global warming may pose a threat to the dry grassland habitat: as temperatures increase, the land could dry out and turn into semiarid or desert landscape. Clearing grassland makes the problem worse, because it leads to soil erosion, which encourages desertification.

Taking over The human population is growing faster than ever. Everyone needs food and a place to live, but this puts increasing pressure on savanna areas. Cities expand onto some grasslands, while others are cleared for crops. Less and less remains for the savanna wildlife.

Tourism Safaris and other forms of tourism bring in much needed money to poor countries, but it comes at a price as hotels degrade the landscape and increase pollution. Also, animals are developing behavioral problems due to stress from being observed for long periods.

Essential elephants The elephant is a "keystone species," which means it plays a vital part in maintaining its particular habitat. Savanna would eventually turn into scrub if it were not for the elephant, which eats woody vegetation and pushes down trees to gain access to the higher branches. But the elephant is a threatened species.

Don't buy items made of ivory, elephant hair, or elephant skin: no matter how small the object is, an elephant still had to die for it to be made.

POACHING

One of the biggest threats to elephants is poaching. Between 1979 and 1989, 600,000 African elephants were killed for their tusks, halving the population in just 10 years.

CONSERVATION

People pose a threat to both the elephant and its habitat. One of the best ways of conserving elephants is to involve local people and convince them of their worth.

LOSS OF LAND

Elephants roam large distances to feed, but their habitat is shrinking as savanna is built upon or turned into farmland. These developments divide up the remaining savanna, cutting through the elephants' ranges.

RAMPAGING

Elephants may wander on to farmland, where they eat and trample crops. This brings them into conflict with local farmers often with fatal consequences for both sides.

CO_2 ••••••••• O_2

be as devastating as felling rain forests.

An unfair target The large animals of Africa also attract a different kind of tourist: hunters who kill for sport. The number of African countries offering shooting licenses is increasing. The argument for doing this is that it raises money to fund conservation.

Poaching Although many animals are protected by law, the continuing demand for them leads to poaching. Tigers are killed for their bones and skins, rhinos for their horns, and elephants for their ivory. Some animals are literally worth their weight in gold.

Cattle ranching Many areas of tropical grassland are being used for ranching. Seventy percent of the llanos, in South America, has been lost over the last 40 years: besides crops, there are now about 15 million cattle there. Very little of the llanos is protected and so ranching continues to expand.

the wildebeest

FOLLOWING THE MASS MIGRATION OF THE HERBIVORES IN THEIR CONTINUAL SEARCH FOR GRASS SHOOTS

Every year, about one and a half million wildebeest migrate a distance of 1,120 miles (1,800 km) to find food. Wildebeest feed on fresh grass shoots, and spend much of the year moving around to find them. The animals live in the Serengeti during the wet season, from December to March; but come the dry season there is not enough freshwater for them to drink or for new grass shoots to grow, so they must move on. The herds head north to Lake Victoria and then onto the Masai Mara. They spend the dry season that lasts from July to October in the Masai Mara, where occasional rainstorms provide enough moisture for the grass to grow. However, this grass lacks nutrients, so as the wet season commences the herds return south once more to eat the phosphorus-rich grass of the Serengeti.

The Serengeti, Lake Victoria, and Masai Mara are all in East Africa. It takes about 3 months to migrate between each place.

The long migration is not without dangers. Many wildebeest slip down steep riverbanks and drown; others are killed crossing the crocodile-infested waters. Hyenas and jackals are also ready to attack the weak and young.

farmland ecosystem

Farmland is not a natural landscape. All land that is used for farming has been converted from another ecosystem, such as prairie, forest, or even desert. Agriculture can change thick woodland to a patchwork of fields that look like they have existed forever—but it's all made by people. In taking over, farming replaces the wild plants and animals with ones that people can control. Most agriculture today is "settled," meaning the soil is fertile enough to support permanent farms.

TOP TEN CROPS

This chart shows how much of each crop is grown around the world in one year. Cereals are by far the biggest harvest because they are used in all kinds of food.

Millions of metric tons

700
600
500
400
300
200
100
0

Corn — Rice — Wheat — Potatoes — Cassava — Soybeans — Sweet potatoes — Barley — Bananas — Sorghum

Dairy cattle eat high-quality pasture to produce nutritious milk. Guernsey cows produce especially rich milk, which is ideal for turning into butter. This breed is not kept for meat.

What's growing? Farmland is used for growing crops (arable agriculture) or raising livestock (pastoralism). While the majority of the world's farmland is arable, many farms are mixed, so if harvests are bad the farmer has income from the livestock, and vice versa.

Plantations are large-scale intensive arable farms. Crops such as tea and bananas are grown on trees and bushes, usually for export.

Intensive or extensive?
Farming practices depend on how much land and money are available. Intensive farming puts a lot of work into a small area of land in order to get a good yield. With extensive farming, the same amount of work is spread out over much more land.

Cereal provider Over half the world's food comes from just three sources: corn, rice, and wheat. Like all cereals, these familiar dinner-table crops are actually grasses. The original wild plants were cultivated to produce edible grains.

CORN
Corn is native to central America. Cultivated corn is totally different to wild corn, which has few, very tough and inedible kernels.

RYE
A close relative of wheat, rye grains are mostly made into flour for bread and crackers. The stalks are also made into corn dollies!

OATS
The most familiar form of oats is as breakfast cereal, including oatmeal and muesli. Horses and cattle eat crushed raw oats as a main part of their diet.

WHEAT
To get to the edible grain inside the husk, wheat must be winnowed, which is traditionally done by tossing wheat into the air.

RICE
This plant originally comes from Asia and Africa, and today it is the staple food of Asia. Rice is the only crop that can be grown in flooded fields.

Comma butterflies feed on a variety of plants. As caterpillars they eat crops such as hops; adult butterflies sip nectar from weeds such as thistles.

Hedgerows and "barrier fields" at the farm's edge provide a home for wild animals and plants displaced by the farm—including harvest mice.

Harvest mice used to make their nests among crops such as wheat, but modern combine harvesters have made crop fields too dangerous for them.

COMMERCIAL
Most farms are commercial, with farmers growing crops or raising animals for sale. The biggest are sheep farms, cattle ranches, and those growing cereals.

SLASH AND BURN
A quarter of the world's population relies on slash-and-burn agriculture, where forests are cleared to make room for crops. When the soil gets exhausted, another area will be felled.

SHIFTING
Also called nomadic, shifting farmers keep on the move so their herds can find enough food to eat. This farming occurs where the land isn't fertile enough to support settled farms.

SPECIALIST
Plantations and other farms that focus on one type of produce are specialized. The crop may be dependent on the area's soil and climate: Mediterranean farms are ideal for olives and vines.

131

aggressive agriculture

There are 2 million species of wild animals and plants in the world, but fewer than 30 kinds of animals and 200 kinds of plants found on farms. In order to get the most out of the farms, there are many agricultural practices that effect the environment. As *valuable* sources of food or materials, the domesticated species are given everything they need to grow, and any competition for resources is soon **gotten rid of**: plants are plowed up or cut down; animals are fenced off the land; and both may be poisoned.

BE AWARE of food miles—know where

Mechanization Tractors and combine harvesters can process crops more efficiently than a team of people by hand. But machines are large, and fields need to be big enough to accommodate them. Expanding fields destroys hedgerows that provide a safe corridor and a home for wildlife.

Factory farming It is unnatural to force animals to produce lots of meat, milk, or eggs rapidly or to breed every season, but factory farming does just that. Packed into pens with little room to exercise, piglets are fed concentrates and hormones to fatten them up fast so they can be taken to market sooner.

Chemical treatments Pesticides are used to kill bugs that eat crops, but they also kill other wildlife, and pass into the food chain. Fertilizers help crops grow in fields, but when rain washes the fertilizer into rivers, plants spring to life in the water too, choking the river and the wildlife within it.

Chain reaction Land converted from forests and prairies to farmland is not just ideal for fields— it's also a clear, accessible place to build new communities to cope with a growing population. But these extra people need food, too, and if housing developments are built on farmland, where will the food come from? More farms will need to be created, and more prairies and forests will be lost.

your food comes from.

Food miles Importing food such as fruit and vegetables by plane or boat creates pollution. Transporting livestock is also distressing for the animals.

Look for the "country of origin" label on food. Was your apple grown locally, or has it been flown across the world?

Biofuel There's currently a big demand for "biofuel"—fuel that comes from plant sources rather than minerals such as oil. As fields are given over to rape or soybean crops that provide this fuel, there's less land for growing food. So more fields need to be created, taking land from other ecosystems.

Methane Rice fields, or paddies, are flooded for four months a year. During this time, rice stems rot in the water and release methane into the air. It is thought that wet paddies are the largest man-made source of methane, which is a greenhouse gas that contributes to global warming.

controversial crops

People have always tried to *improve* the food they grow. In the past this was done by taking seeds from only the best plants so that the next year's crops would inherit good qualities. Those that were too small or tasteless or prone to disease wouldn't be used for seeds. **Genetic modification** is different. Scientists alter the actual genes of a plant, perhaps to make them toxic to insects or herbicide-resistant.

Flavr Savr tomato   Golden rice   Soybeans   Rape seed

GM gallery The first GM crop grown for sale was the Flavr Savr tomato, made to be resistant to rot so it kept fresh in stores for longer. Today the most widely grown GM crops are oilseed rape, used in cooking oil and biofuels, and soybeans, used in lots of processed foods and animal feed. These crops were modified to help the farmer grow them more efficiently, but other crop modifications may be aimed at the consumer: Golden rice has added Vitamin A to boost the diet of people in poor countries.

GM is still quite new—no one can say if

FOR GM

LESS PESTICIDE
"Bt cotton" has been modified to be toxic to bollworms, pests that eat the plant. Now the farmer doesn't have to spray pesticide over the crops to kill the destructive bollworm caterpillars.

HERBICIDE-RESISTANT CROPS
Fields can be sprayed with very effective herbicides that kill everything but the crop. Without weeds competing for sunlight, water, and nutrients, crop yields will be higher.

A VARIETY OF FARMS
GM crops can be grown alongside other types of crop and there is no evidence to date that they damage the environment directly.

TACKLING CLIMATE CHANGE
Crops can be engineered to cope with harsh, dry, or salty conditions created by climate change, or to increase the health benefits of food to improve the diets of people living in poor countries.

SAFE FOR ANIMALS
Cows, chickens, and pigs are already eating large quantities of GM produce without showing any ill effects. Much of their feed is made from GM soybeans, which are cheaper to grow than non-GM.

AGAINST GM

BUT...
Over time, bollworms could evolve to have resistance to the toxin, which may also damage beneficial insects, such as the monarch butterfly. The farmer may have to spray pesticides to deal with other pests anyway.

BUT...
Growing herbicide-resistant crops is bad for other farmland wildlife. Weeds and their seeds provide vital food for insects and birds. If the food disappears, there will be fewer animals, and this will upset the whole food chain.

BUT...
Pollen from GM crops can spread their modified genes into other crops and wild plants. Organic farmers nearby cannot guarantee that their food is free from GM genes, so they lose their organic status.

BUT...
Companies that develop GM seeds focus on varieties that will make them the best profit. They are unlikely to help poor farmers in marginal areas.

BUT...
We don't know if people will suffer side effects in the long-term from eating GM foods, either directly or through eating produce from animals fed on GM. Non-GM foods have been proven over centuries to be safe.

it will lead to problems in the future.

MAKING A DIFFERENCE

How does your GARDEN grow?

* **Lawns are grasslands, too,** and it's important not to pave over them. Avoid using herbicide on the grass so wildflowers can grow and attract wildlife.

* **Keep a patch of grass long** and watch the wildlife take shelter. You might see insects, birds, frogs, hedgehogs, and even badgers.

* **Make a compost heap** and use the compost to fertilize flower beds. It's the ultimate in efficient recycling!

Feed your compost with fruit and vegetable peelings, used teabags, and grass clippings.

Wild flowers love long lawns

what you can do

Is there a grassland (such as a park, open space, or Green Belt land) in your area that's under threat? Start or join a campaign to protect it.

Dear Representative Smith,

I have seen in my local newspaper that developers want to build houses on an area of Green Belt grassland. I am writing to ask that you do not let this happen.

Grassland needs to be protected. Some species of animals and plants will die out if this land is lost, and people will also lose their breathing spaces outside of town.

Grass also helps to combat global warming because it helps to absorb CO_2. If grasslands are destroyed, we lose this benefit, and the problem is made worse because the new houses would create even more pollution. Please preserve our natural open spaces.

Yours sincerely,

Sam Green

Write a letter

write a letter to your Congressperson to show that you care!

From providing animals with homes and food to helping combat global warming, grasslands are the planet's unsung heroes.

African elephant mother and calf, Masai Mara, Africa

Black rhino mother and calf, Tanzania, Africa

what you can do

Think about where you buy your food. Support local stores and cut down on pollution by walking or taking the bus rather than the car.

what you can do

Adopt an animal to help save endangered species such as elephants, rhinos, leopards, and lions. Many charities do this, including WWF: www.wwf.org

KNOW THE DEBATE:

local food

- **Local food never has to travel very far,** so it doesn't use much energy in transportation. This helps cut down on pollution.
- Because it takes less time to get from field to store, **local food is likely to be fresher,** and so there is less need for large amounts of refrigeration or packaging to protect it, which take a lot of energy to produce.
- Buying locally **supports your local economy and provides jobs for local farmers.**
- Local food helps you learn about **where your food comes from and what your own country can produce.**
- **BUT local food may be produced using environmentally polluting farming methods,** such as herbicides, pesticides, and fertilizers.

organic food

- Grown in harmony with the environment, organic food has **no pesticides, herbicides, or other chemical fertilizers.**
- These chemicals take a lot of energy to manufacture. By not using them, organic farming uses a lot less energy overall than conventional food production.
- **Organic farms support more birds, mammals, insects, and wild flowers.**
- **Organic farms are kinder to their animals**—cows are cared for, pigs are not packed into pens, and chickens are uncaged. They are never given hormones or unnecessary drugs to boost production.
- **BUT not many farms produce organic food,** so it often has to be imported from far-away countries to meet demand. This creates extra "food miles," and increases carbon emissions.

TROPICAL FORESTS

Tropical **forests** grow near the *equator*. The constant **heat** and high rainfall helps *trees* grow tall.

Some forests have rain all year. Some are only wet for part of the year. Others get the moisture they need from clouds. They are all shrinking, as humans cut them down for lumber, or to open up the land beneath the trees. Changing climate could cause even more problems.

TROPICAL FORESTS

where on earth...?

Tropical forests grow throughout the tropical zone close to the equator, wherever it is wet enough for trees to grow (savanna grasslands or deserts are found in drier areas). The type of forest depends on how much it rains and how often.

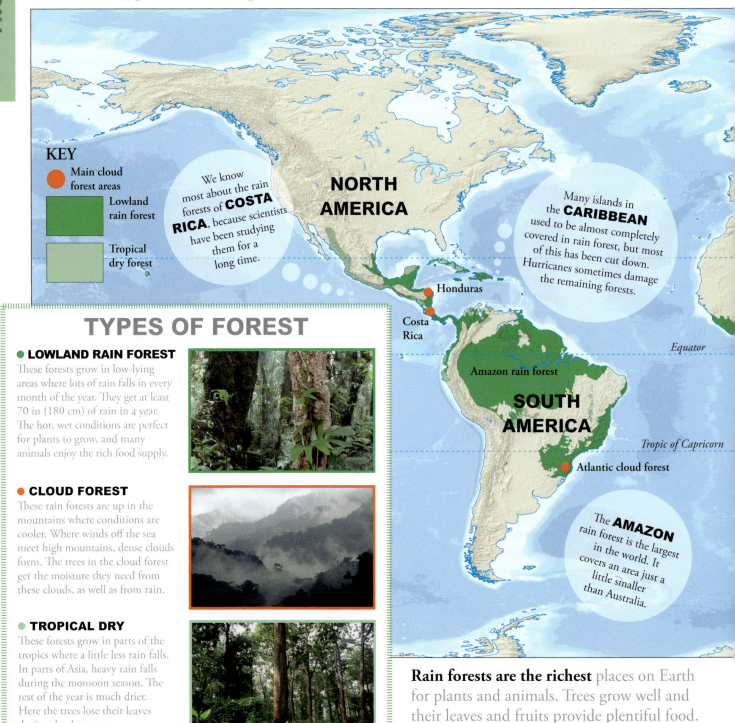

KEY

🔴 Main cloud forest areas

🟩 Lowland rain forest

⬜ Tropical dry forest

We know most about the rain forests of **COSTA RICA**, because scientists have been studying them for a long time.

NORTH AMERICA

Many islands in the **CARIBBEAN** used to be almost completely covered in rain forest, but most of this has been cut down. Hurricanes sometimes damage the remaining forests.

Honduras

Costa Rica

Equator

Amazon rain forest

SOUTH AMERICA

Tropic of Capricorn

Atlantic cloud forest

The **AMAZON** rain forest is the largest in the world. It covers an area just a little smaller than Australia.

TYPES OF FOREST

🟢 **LOWLAND RAIN FOREST**

These forests grow in low-lying areas where lots of rain falls in every month of the year. They get at least 70 in (180 cm) of rain in a year. The hot, wet conditions are perfect for plants to grow, and many animals enjoy the rich food supply.

🟠 **CLOUD FOREST**

These rain forests are up in the mountains where conditions are cooler. Where winds off the sea meet high mountains, dense clouds form. The trees in the cloud forest get the moisture they need from these clouds, as well as from rain.

🟢 **TROPICAL DRY**

These forests grow in parts of the tropics where a little less rain falls. In parts of Asia, heavy rain falls during the monsoon season. The rest of the year is much drier. Here the trees lose their leaves during the dry season.

Rain forests are the richest places on Earth for plants and animals. Trees grow well and their leaves and fruits provide plentiful food. However, plants cannot grow if their leaves are eaten as soon as they appear, so many rain

WHERE'S THE JUNGLE?

Rain forests and other tropical forests are sometimes called jungles, but thick "walls" of plants only appear along the riverbanks. Inside, the forest can be fairly open.

ALWAYS SUMMER

In rain forests and cloud forests, it is warm and wet all year. In these conditions plants can grow and produce fruits and flowers all through the year. This ensures a constant supply of food for animals.

LOSING LEAVES

In monsoon forests, the wet season is like summer. When the dry season comes, most trees shed their leaves to stop them from losing water. The dry season is like winter in other parts of the world.

AIR FRESHENER

The many trees and other plants of the tropical forests give out huge amounts of oxygen. All animals rely on oxygen to live and these forests have been described as the "lungs of the world."

VANISHING FORESTS

Many tropical forests produce valuable lumber, so people cut them down. In the future, more rain forests will die if climate change leads to less rain falling on them.

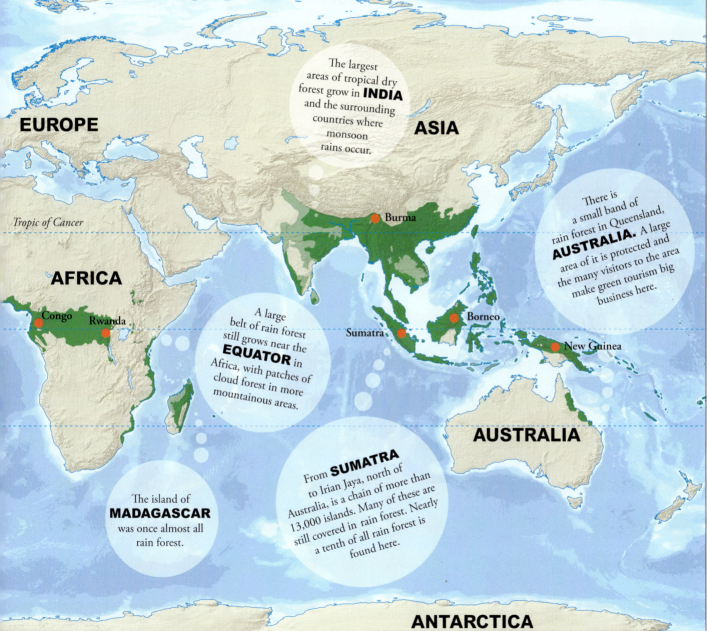

The largest areas of tropical dry forest grow in **INDIA** and the surrounding countries where monsoon rains occur.

There is a small band of rain forest in Queensland, **AUSTRALIA.** A large area of it is protected and the many visitors to the area make green tourism big business here.

A large belt of rain forest still grows near the **EQUATOR** in Africa, with patches of cloud forest in more mountainous areas.

The island of **MADAGASCAR** was once almost all rain forest.

From **SUMATRA** to Irian Jaya, north of Australia, is a chain of more than 13,000 islands. Many of these are still covered in rain forest. Nearly a tenth of all rain forest is found here.

forest plants have leaves containing nasty chemicals to stop animals from eating them. Some animals have developed clever means of getting round these defenses—and to keep other animals from eating them! Over thousands of years, this constant battle to eat or be eaten has made plants and animals change, as they have found new ways to live. Many changed so much they became new species. This battle for life is why so many different kinds of plants and animals are found here.

lowland rain forest

Lowland rain forest is the largest tropical rain-forest ecosystem. It is hot all year round and more than 70 in (180 cm) of rain falls during the year. In the warm, wet climate trees grow very tall. The forest forms three layers—an evergreen canopy in the middle, a layer of smaller plants on the forest floor, and scattered taller trees towering above the canopy.

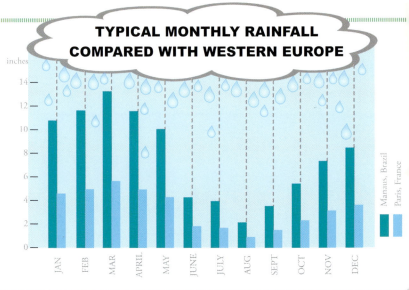

TYPICAL MONTHLY RAINFALL COMPARED WITH WESTERN EUROPE

inches

Manaus, Brazil
Paris, France

JAN FEB MAR APRIL MAY JUNE JULY AUG SEPT OCT NOV DEC

This toucan uses its colorful beak to crack open fruits and gobble up insects.

Caimans stalk the many rivers that flow through the rain forest. They use their powerful jaws to grab animals that have come to the river for a drink and drag them out into the depths to drown.

Few plants grow on the shady rain-forest floor. Most scramble upward to reach the sunlight high above.

Caiman

Chemical warfare With so many grazing animals around, many trees have developed poisons in their leaves to stop animals from eating them. However, some animals, like these mealy parrots, get around this by eating clay from the riverbanks. The clay lines their stomach and absorbs the poisons from the leaves.

LEAPING LIZARDS

Many lizards live high in the treetops and some of them have flaps of skin along their bodies. They can spread these out to glide from tree to tree.

ecosystem

Rain forest food chain Huge numbers of plants and animals live in the different layers of the forest, from the high, leafy canopy to the shady forest floor far below.

Plants

Squirrel monkey

Eagle

Jaguar

Fungi

PRODUCERS
Many plants perch high on the branches of big trees. This keeps them near the sunlight they need for energy.

PRIMARY CONSUMERS
Monkeys, sloths, birds, and insects all munch on the huge amounts of leaves and fruits.

SECONDARY CONSUMERS
The leaf-eaters fall prey to many hunters, ranging from anteaters to hawks, owls, and eagles.

TOP CARNIVORES
The hunters themselves get killed and eaten by a few top predators, like jaguars or the anaconda snakes that live in rivers or along river banks.

DECOMPOSERS
On the warm, wet forest floor fungi, termites, and beetles get rid of any animal and plant remains.

Many forest animals spend almost all their lives high up in the trees, and scarcely ever come to the ground. Gibbons like this can climb, swing, or leap through the treetop highway.

Rain-forest trees have massive root systems that help to hold the trees up in the thin soil.

JEEPERS CREEPERS
Lianas are climbing plants. They grow up from the ground, hang onto branches with suckers, then spread among the treetops. Their long roots dangle down to the soil below.

PEOPLE OF THE TREES
The rain forest provides food for native people as well as medicine from trees and plants. Quinine, which is used to treat malaria, comes from the cinchona tree.

FLOWER FESTIVAL
In lowland rain forest, it is "summer" all year round, so trees can flower at any time. Somewhere in the forest you will find a tree in flower in every month of the year.

HOT HOUSES
Several plants that we commonly grow in pots in our houses come originally from the rain forest, like this Monstera. They like the heat in our buildings and do well as long as they are watered regularly.

vanishing rain forest

The rain forest of the **Amazon** basin is the largest *tropical* rain forest in the world. It covers **2.3 million** sq miles (6 million sq km)—an area almost as big as **Australia**. It holds around a **fifth** of all *flowering plant species* in the world, a **fifth** of all **bird species** and *one in ten* mammals. Huge areas of the forest are being **cleared and burned** to make way for **cattle ranching** or farmland.

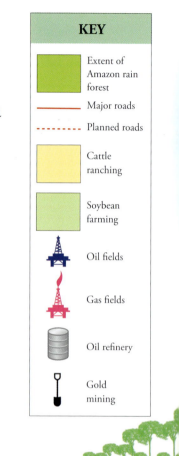

KEY

Extent of Amazon rain forest

Major roads

Planned roads

Cattle ranching

Soybean farming

Oil fields

Gas fields

Oil refinery

Gold mining

Although tree felling is illegal in many areas, it is not possible to police the whole forest and stop the loggers.

Slum city Around 20 million people live in the Amazon region. Manaus has a population of 1.4 million, with many living in slums by the river. This leads to pollution of the waterways. The local forest is used to provide food and firewood.

Illegal lumber In such a poor country, the high price fetched by lumber is a huge temptation. Local people fell trees at night, then drag them to riverbanks. They cut many small trees to get to the best lumber trees. Boats later collect the lumber piles.

Bad burgers Large areas of forest have been cleared to create grasslands, where cattle herds now graze. The meat is exported to North America to make hamburgers. With no trees, the soil is poor and streams dry up in the hottest season.

The map of the Amazon basin shows where people have cleared large areas in the once continuous Amazon forest.

Around a sixth of the Amazon rain forest has already been destroyed. In 2004, 10,000 sq miles (26,000 sq km), an area bigger than Wales, was cleared. New roads have been built that have opened up other areas, allowing people to get in there more easily to fell more trees. More forest is being cleared to grow soybeans or graze cattle, for oilfields, gold mining, and dams. The populations of cities such as Manaus and Belem have grown very fast as rural people move to them for a better life. Felling so much rain forest has had an effect on local weather as the trees give out a lot of moisture. The climate is becoming drier and this in turn is killing more trees.

VENEZUELA
GUYANA
COLOMBIA
SURINAME
FRENCH GUIANA
ECUADOR
THE ANDES
Belem
Manaus
BRAZIL
PERU
BOLIVIA
CHILE
PARAGUAY

The Amazon River provides a highway right into the forest, making it possible to get into it to fell trees.

So much for soybeans

Soybeans grow well in the poor, dry soils that are left when the rain forest is cleared. In Brazil, the area farmed for soybeans has doubled in recent years. Half the crop is shipped to Europe, where it is used to feed chicken and pigs.

Poison in the water

Gold was discovered in the 1980s in parts of the Amazon basin opened up by the new Transamazon highway. The poisonous metal mercury is used to extract the gold. The waste drains into rivers and enters the food chain.

Green business

It is not all bad news! More wealthy tourists are visiting the Amazon to enjoy its natural wonders and friendly people. Outdoor centers are being set up to help visitors explore the rain forest. This shows the forest is worth saving.

the orangutan

PALM OIL IS A VALUABLE CROP IN BORNEO, BUT ITS PLANTATIONS ARE DESTROYING THE HOME OF THE ORANGUTAN

In Borneo, an area of forest the size of 180 football fields is cut down every hour to make way for palm-oil plantations. This leaves smaller and smaller patches of forest where orangutans can live. Only 25,000 of them remain, and at this rate they could all die out within 10 years. Now people want to grow even more oil palms to make biofuels (fuel made from plant sources). About 80 percent of the world's production of palm-oil biofuel comes from areas that were once covered by rain forests in Malaysia and Indonesia. Biofuels help the environment by slowing climate change, but at the expense of the orangutan and its home.

Orangutans live in rain forests on the islands of Sumatra and Borneo. Scientists think these are two different species.

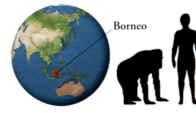

Borneo

Since 1980, large parts of the forests where orangutans live have been felled by people in order to plant oil palms. Oil from the fruits of these palm trees is used to make many popular goods such as ice cream, chocolate, potato chips, cookies, margarine, toothpaste, soap, and cosmetics.

Palm oil

Palm fruit

Read the label and try to avoid products that use palm oil. If you can, find an organic alternative, because no rain forest will have been felled to make it.

cloud forest ecosystem

Cloud forest is a form of rain forest that grows between 6,500 and 11,500 ft (2,000–3,500 m) up in tropical mountains. Winds full of moisture from the sea are forced upwards when they hit the mountains. As it is cooler higher up, moisture comes out of the air to form clouds. The clouds make the forest dripping wet, even when it is not raining, but they also hide the Sun.

Clouds hang almost constantly over these forests, which are also called montane rain forests.

The emerald toucanet uses its large bill to dig holes in trees for its nest and to eat berries.

The blue morpho butterfly feeds mainly on the juices of rotting fruits on the forest floor, where it spends most of its life. However, in the breeding season it flies into the forest canopy to find a mate.

Mountain gorillas, like this baby, live in cloud forests in the mountains of central Africa.

Forest-covered mountains in Democratic Republic of Congo and Rwanda are the home of the mountain gorilla. A male gorilla weighs twice as much as a human, yet this big beast lives entirely on leaves, shoots, and stems gathered from the forest floor. He is too heavy to climb trees.

GORILLA GROUP

Family groups of gorillas move into clearings in the forest to feed. Younger animals climb trees to find fruit. A big male can eat 65 lbs (30 kg) of plants a day.

Richness in numbers The Monteverde cloud forest in Costa Rica, Central America, has been studied in detail by many scientists. They have found amazing numbers of plants and animals there.

Heliconius butterfly

Golden mantella frog

Ocelot

Tree-dwelling orchid

Imperial eagle

BUTTERFLIES
Scientists have found more than 500 different species of butterflies living in the 19 sq miles (50 sq kms) of protected nature reserve in Monteverde.

AMPHIBIANS
The damp conditions on the forest floor suit amphibians perfectly. Monteverde is home to 120 species of amphibians and reptiles.

MAMMALS
There are 100 species of mammals in Monteverde, including the ocelot. This shy cat hunts small mammals on the forest floor at night.

PLANTS
The ever-damp conditions support 2,500 plant species, including this orchid that lives on forest tree branches high above the ground.

BIRDS
Many birds pass through Monteverde as they migrate between North and South America. More than 400 species of birds have been recorded.

Clouds block the sunshine but bring plenty of water to the forest. The Monteverde forest gets 118 in (300 cm) of rain in a year. Trees grow shorter and more twisted in these conditions.

The mountain sipo snake has no poisonous fangs. It hunts small birds and mammals.

VOLCANIC LIVING
Mountain gorillas live above 10,000 ft (3,000 m) in protected cloud forest on the slopes of volcanoes that lie between Rwanda and Uganda in central Africa.

RIVER RUNNER
The plumed basilisk lizard lives beside cloud-forest ponds. When danger threatens, it can run across the water, helped by the hairy fringes on its toes.

MOSSY WORLD
Cloud-forest trees grow shorter and more twisted than those in rain forests. In the constant dampness, lichens and mosses flourish.

POKEY COATI
The coati is a mongoose-sized animal from South America. It uses its long, flexible nose to poke around among the dead leaves on the forest floor to find worms and other insects.

trouble in the clouds

Cloud forests are under threat. In areas where people are *poor* and short of **food** they have cut down the trees to make cheap fuel and to create space to grow crops, especially on islands in the **Caribbean** like Cuba and Trinidad. Today cloud forests survive mainly on *higher, steeper* slopes that are not so easily accessible.

Fruit bats move around the forest to find ripe fruits. If climate change affects fruiting times, that may cause problems for bats feeding.

Cloud forests are being cut down, and

Hurricane alley Scientists think that climate change is causing bigger hurricanes to happen more often. The shape of cloud forests generally protects them from hurricanes, but, where they have been opened up by felling, the winds can cause serious damage.

Drip tip Many leaves of cloud-forest trees end in a long point called a drip tip, which allows rain to run off and stops damaging fungi from growing all over their surface. This adaptation shows how well designed they are for ever-wet conditions, but it makes them very sensitive to dry weather.

Tree hitchhiker Many plants, like this orchid, grow perched on the branches of cloud-forest trees. They get the moisture and nutrients they need from clouds and rain. Climate change may cause them real problems as nine out of 10 plants in the Monteverde cloud forest cannot stand being dry for long periods.

EL NIÑO

Every 3–5 years, the cold current off the coast of South America is replaced by unusually warm water at the sea surface. This event is called *El Niño* ("the boy child") since it happens at Christmastime. Although *El Niño* arises off the coast of Peru, its effect is widespread in the Pacific. In Central America, the winds off the sea die away, so no clouds form over the mountains. The wet season becomes shorter and drier, many plants cannot flower, and animals fail to breed. *El Niño* is a natural event and the forest survives, but climate change is making *El Niño* events more severe and possibly more frequent.

LIFE-GIVING CLOUDS
Cloud forests rely on winds off the sea. These bring clouds to the mountains during the dry season, when it rains very little, and torrential storms during the rainy season. In *El Niño* years, the clouds and rain disappear (right) and the forest becomes drier. Toads and other wet-loving creatures suffer from the dry conditions.

The forest can cope with these changes, provided they do not happen too often.

climate change affects the forests that are left.

Lowland invader As it becomes drier and warmer in the mountains, some lowland species are moving upward into the cloud forest. Birds like this keel-billed toucan could not breed in the forest when it was always wet, but have now begun breeding higher up in the mountain forests.

Locals in trouble As lowland birds get more common in the cloud forest, they eat up large quantities of fruit and other food. That leaves much less for the native birds, like this resplendent quetzal. It relies so much on fruit that it moves through the forest to catch trees as they start fruiting.

Hot fields In Costa Rica, more and more wild countryside is being made into farmland. This makes the land warmer as dark soil absorbs heat and there are no cooling trees. The warming land forces drier winds higher up the mountains, reducing the thickness of cloud cover.

the golden toad

NO ONE WILL EVER SEE A SIGHT LIKE THIS AGAIN AS HOTTER, DRIER CONDITIONS HAVE WIPED OUT THE GOLDEN TOAD

Golden toads relied on the wet cloud forest. They hid in the damp forest floor until the rainy season, then moved to ponds to breed. In 1986 and 1987, their breeding period from April to June was drier and hotter than scientists had ever known before. Perhaps this was an early sign of climate change. In one area where 30,000 toads once lived, only 29 survived the dry spell. A few golden toads were found the next year, but none have been seen since 1989. Scientists think they are extinct. The golden toads are not alone. Twenty other kinds of frogs and toads also died out in Monteverde over the same period.

Costa Rica

The golden toad was only ever found at about 6,500 ft (2,000 m) in the Monteverde cloud forest of Costa Rica.

Female golden toads were dark brown, marked with red and orange blotches. At the start of the rainy season, they gathered round ponds to lay eggs. A golden-colored male hopped on top of the female to fertilize her eggs, so they could become tadpoles. The eggs were then left in the ponds to hatch.

tropical dry forest

Many tropical dry forests are dry only in comparison with rain forests. Monsoon forests have regular thunderstorms with heavy rain during the wet season, when moisture-laden winds blow off the sea. But for part of the year they are very dry. Other forests in southern Africa and South America are truly dry, with little rainfall all year.

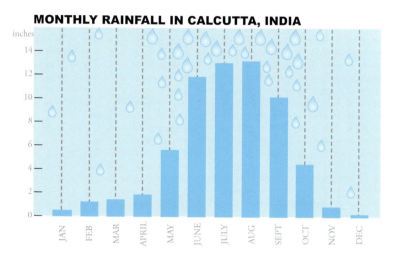

MONTHLY RAINFALL IN CALCUTTA, INDIA

inches: 14, 12, 10, 8, 6, 4, 2, 0

JAN, FEB, MAR, APRIL, MAY, JUNE, JULY, AUG, SEPT, OCT, NOV, DEC

Monsoon seasons

In summer, strong winds blow from the cool sea toward the hot land carrying lots of rain into the forest (far left). When winter comes, the land cools down and the wind blows off it, so it becomes very dry. Little rain falls and the trees begin to shed their leaves (left).

A monsoon forest food chain Food is abundant during the wet season, but scarce during dry times.

Langur monkey

Wildlife flourishes in the trees and on the forest floor.

Reticulated python

Bengal tiger

White-backed vulture

PRODUCERS
Plants grow lushly through the monsoon season. They produce flowers and then fruits, so there is plenty of food for animals.

PRIMARY CONSUMERS
Many monkeys, like these langur monkeys, live in the monsoon forest. They eat leaves off the trees and fruits when available.

SECONDARY CONSUMERS
Reticulated pythons are treetop hunters. They coil up on a branch and wait for a small monkey to come too close.

TOP CARNIVORES
Pigs, deer, and antelopes are the main food of the tiger, but it will hunt monkeys if they come to the ground—and even an occasional python.

SCAVENGERS
Vultures are the forest garbage men, clearing up the remains of all dead animals. They sit in trees or glide above the forest, looking out for their next meal.

Plants grow very little during the dry season, especially if they have shed their leaves. Tropical dry forests are therefore more open than rain forests. Branches provide perching places even for large birds like the Indian peafowl.

Monkeys, like this langur, live mostly high in the trees. Langurs can leap 16 ft (5 m) between branches.

These chital, or spotted deer, live in open areas of the forest. Their spots help hide them from hunters in the sunlight that dapples the forest floor.

WET "DRY" FORESTS

Some monsoon forests get 11 ft (3.5 m) of rain in just four months of monsoon. That means just over an inch (3 cm) of rain falls in a day, mostly in torrential showers.

DRY FLOWERING

Some monsoon forest trees flower during the dry season, when they have no leaves. This timing lets them spread their seeds in the wet season, when they will grow best.

ELEPHANTS IN MOPANE

Elephants are at home in the Mopane forest, which covers a huge area in drier parts of Africa, near the equator. This open, scrubby woodland is halfway to savanna.

AFRO-MONTANE FOREST

Other kinds of tropical forest are dry all year round, but get just enough rain or mist for trees to grow. Afro-montane forest like this is found in upland areas of Africa.

disappearing **dry forests**

Almost all tropical dry forest is found where **people** are desperately poor and struggle to survive. In *African* forest areas, many people rely on wood to cook food and boil water to **drink**, but that means the **trees soon disappear**. In the monsoon forests of Asia farming began many centuries ago. Great areas have been *burned* and *cleared* to make way for fields.

Burning logs helps people live, but soon kills the forest.

Support charities in Africa that are helping people plant trees, so they can grow firewood for the future.

The greatest threat to tropical dry forests

Ox in danger A forest ox called the kouprey was discovered by scientists in the monsoon forests of eastern Asia in 1937. It is greatly in danger because of hunting and clearance of its forest home. None have been seen in the wild since 1988.
A few kouprey, like this one, live in zoos.

Valuable lumber Teak trees produce the finest lumber in the monsoon forests. The hard and long-lasting wood is very valuable and many teak trees are still felled illegally. It can take more than a century for a new tree to grow, so we need to value teak as much as we do gold and protect its forests carefully.

Chopping the chaco The chaco, or Great Thorn Forest, once covered vast areas of South America but much of it has been destroyed. Trees were used for building or as fuel for sugar refineries. Cattle ranching destroyed more trees and now more chaco is being cleared for soybean farming.

Two kinds of dry forest, known locally as the Miombo and Mopane woodlands, cover more than 1 million sq miles (over 3 million sq km) near the equator in central Africa. Over 71 million people live in poverty in the same region, with less than the price of a candy bar per day to live on. The only way they can afford fuel is by collecting wood from the forest. Each person uses about a ton of firewood a year and, at that rate, the forest will be cleared within 100 years.

This woman is collecting firewood to provide the fuel she needs for her family to survive. Behind her, you can see how the forest is disappearing and being turned into dry grassland and desert.

around the world is human poverty.

Spiny climber As the chaco has disappeared, so have its inhabitants, like the Brazilian prehensile-tailed porcupine. It lives in trees and uses its specially adapted tail to wrap around a branch so it can hang as it feeds on leaves and bark. It often moves over half a mile (700 m) a night in search of food.

Not so much sloth The sloth bear lives in tropical dry forests in India and Nepal. It feeds on insects called termites, honey, and birds' eggs. The destruction of forests means that today only a tenth of India's forests are large enough to offer it a safe home, and only 6,000–11,000 sloth bears remain.

Silver survivor The silver tree is one of the special species found in the Afro-montane forest. It grows only on the slopes of Table Mountain and Lion's Head, a neighboring hill, right on the outskirts of Cape Town in South Africa. It is now a protected species—although that does not save it from fires.

the aye-aye

THE SPOOKY-LOOKING AYE-AYE LIVES IN THE FORESTS OF MADAGASCAR, BUT THESE ARE DISAPPEARING FAST

Although Madagascar is close to Africa, it has been separate for a long time, so many animals living there are found nowhere else. The aye-aye is a kind of lemur or early monkey. It hunts at night for insects, using its big ears to track them down and its long fingers to winkle them out from beneath the bark of trees. Sometimes it uses its extra-long middle finger to scoop the flesh out of coconuts or other fruits, like we would use a long ice-cream spoon. As forests are destroyed, the aye-aye is becoming extremely rare. Nobody knows how many are left, but there are probably fewer than 2,500 of them.

A few zoos are trying to breed aye-ayes in cages to make sure some survive. Find out if you can visit one of these zoos. Your entry fee will help their work.

Madagascar

Madagascar is the fourth biggest island in the world. It is a bit larger than France.

Many people live on Madagascar and its forests are being cut and then burned to clear land for farming. Three-quarters of the forest has already gone, and the rest could be destroyed within 50 years, along with all the animals that live there, including the aye-aye.

159

MAKING A DIFFERENCE

FRIENDS OF THE FOREST

* **The Fairtrade Association** makes sure small farmers in developing countries get fair prices for their products.
* **World Wide Fund for Nature** works to protect tropical forests and rare species like the Bengal tiger.
. * **Forest Stewardship Council** helps people to buy tropical lumber wisely.

Save the Bengal tiger

Bird-friendly coffee

Coffee was once grown beneath trees. Many new kinds are grown in open sunshine, so trees go and birds lose their homes. Buy shade-grown coffee to help the birds.

Shade-grown coffee beans

what you can do

ADOPT-AN-ACRE. Sponsor an acre of rain forest for yourself to help keep it safe. www.worldlandtrust.org

8   THE DAILY NEWS

GARDEN FURNITURE FOR SALE

BUY WISELY
FSC APPROVED

NOT CHEAP BUT NOT TEAK
DURABLE AND ECO-FRIENDLY

EXTRA COMFORT AT AFFORDABLE PRICE
NO RAIN FOREST DESTROYED

MADE FROM SUSTAINABLE FOREST

Look for furniture with the Forest Stewardship Council logo, showing it has come from forests that are being looked after for the future. Over 5 million acres (2 million hectares) of forest in Bolivia have become FSC certified. This helps to protect important areas of the Amazon rain forest. Certified wood from these forests is being sold by leading do-it-yourself stores in Europe and America.

Rain forest-friendly furniture

Teak and mahogany from tropical forests offer long-lasting lumber for lawn furniture. But if we buy them unwisely, we contribute to the destruction of the forests.

Green tourism shows local people the value of their forest. If you get a chance, take a jungle vacation and explore the rain forest.

what you can do

Learn what food comes from rain forest areas and try to buy products that have been grown in a responsible way.

RAIN FOREST-FRIENDLY SHOPPING

- Fair-trade coffee
- Fair-trade chocolate
- local meat
- organic palm-oil products
- organic soybeans

Oil palm

Along the Amazon, local people earn cash taking tourists out to photograph caimans at night. The animals are later released.

Organic chips

HELP PROTECT MOUNTAIN GORILLAS

Mountain gorillas are one of the rarest cloud-forest animals: there may only be 700 of them left in the wild. Several conservation charities have got together as the International Gorilla Conservation Program to help to save them. They are working with the governments of the Democratic Republic of the Congo, Rwanda, and Congo, and with local people, to look after the forest. They employ rangers to guard the animals from poachers, and to welcome visitors who come to see the gorillas. Visit www.igcp.org for the latest news about the gorilla program.

what you can do

Help protect orangutans by supporting the WWF's "Heart of Borneo Program." Go to www.panda.org

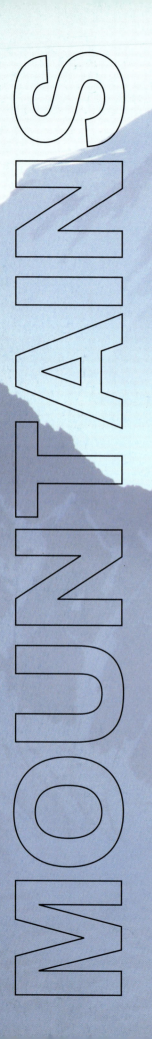

MOUNTAINS

Mountains and highlands are *tough places* to live. They have severe weather and **poor**, *rocky* soils.

In many ways they are like the polar regions. Temperatures drop very low at night and in winter. Winds are strong, and often bring snow. Only plants and animals that are specially adapted can survive such bitter conditions.

MOUNTAINS AND HIGHLANDS

where on earth...?

Mountains are high hills rising well above the surrounding land. There is no exact height at which land becomes a mountain, although generally high land is more than 1,650 ft (500 m) above sea level and most mountains are above 6,500 ft (2,000 m).

Mount McKinley
20,320 ft (6,194 m)

ROCKY MOUNTAINS

NORTH AMERICA

Colorado Plateau

ROCKY MOUNTAINS

Tropic of Cancer

ATLA

MOUNT MCKINLEY in the Denali National Park, Alaska, is the highest point in North America.

From its base on the ocean floor, **MAUNA KEA** in Hawaii is the world's tallest mountain. It rises 33,000 ft (10,000 m), although only 13,796 ft (4,205 m) is above sea level.

CERRO ACONCAGUA is the tallest mountain outside the Himalayas, and the highest in South America.

ANDES

SOUTH AMERICA

Equator

Tropic of Capricorn

Cerro Aconcagua
22,834 ft
(6,959 m)

ANDES

VINSON MASSIF is the highest of the Antarctic mountains that stick out above the ice sheet.

Vinson Massif
16,066 ft (4,897 m) ▲

Mount Everest, the highest point on Earth

Here, January temperatures drop as low as -76°F (-60°C), and the warmest daytime temperature in July is around 3.2°F (-16°C). Winds commonly reach over 100 mph (160 km/h). No animal lives at its summit, although a few birds may visit in summer.

ARCTIC LINKS

Mountain plants and animals face weather that's very similar to the Arctic. Some plant species are found in both areas—scientists and gardeners call these plants "arctic alpines." Some mountain animals also live in the Arctic.

WEATHER EFFECT

Mountain weather depends on the climate of the surrounding area. Mount Kilimanjaro is close to the Equator where it is hot. There trees grow at 10,000 ft (3,000 m). In Scandinavia, where it is cold, mountains that high are snow covered all year.

HIGH LIVING

Plants and animals live at different heights up a mountain depending on the weather. So a plant that lives at 10,000 ft (3,000 m) in the warmth of the Alps, lives a third as high in the Scottish mountains, and beside the sea in Alaska or Greenland.

SPOT THE HEIGHT

The exact height of a mountain is difficult to measure. In 1953 Mount Everest was estimated at 29,028 ft (8,848 m) high. In 1999, Americans using satellites decided it was seven feet taller, but a later survey reduced it to 29,016 ft (8,844 m).

LONE PEAK

Although Mount Everest is the world's highest point, it rises from an area of high land. If you think of a mountain as a cone shape lying on a flat plain, then Mount Kilimanjaro is the tallest mountain, rising 15,990 ft (4,600 m) from the plains below.

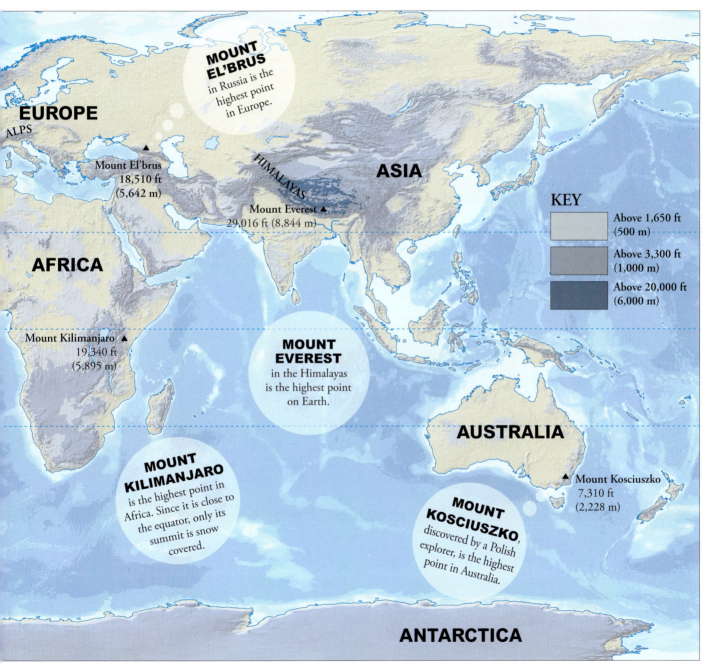

MOUNT EL'BRUS in Russia is the highest point in Europe.

EUROPE

ALPS

Mount El'brus
18,510 ft
(5,642 m)

HIMALAYAS

ASIA

Mount Everest ▲
29,016 ft (8,844 m)

AFRICA

KEY

Above 1,650 ft (500 m)

Above 3,300 ft (1,000 m)

Above 20,000 ft (6,000 m)

Mount Kilimanjaro ▲
19,340 ft
(5,895 m)

MOUNT EVEREST in the Himalayas is the highest point on Earth.

AUSTRALIA

MOUNT KILIMANJARO is the highest point in Africa. Since it is close to the equator, only its summit is snow covered.

Mount Kosciuszko
7,310 ft
(2,228 m)

MOUNT KOSCIUSZKO, discovered by a Polish explorer, is the highest point in Australia.

ANTARCTICA

In 1953 Edmund Hillary and Sherpa Tenzing Norgay were the first to reach the top of Mount Everest.

Mountains and highlands are upland areas that have harsh weather, with strong winds, cold temperatures at night and in winter, and often ice and snow. Since mountains rise more steeply and to greater heights than highlands, they have the worst weather.

mountain ecosystem

In the mountain valleys, plants and animals thrive, but life is very different on the high mountain slopes. Here it is icy cold in winter, and bitterly cold at night. During the day, the Sun warms the slopes, but at night the thin air above the peaks lets heat escape quickly. In winter, when the Sun is farthest away and wind and snow whip the icy ground, very few plants and animals survive.

Average monthly temperature on Mt. Washington 6,289 ft (1,917 m)

High on Mount Washington, daily temperatures only creep above freezing for five months of the year.

(Chart temperature axis, top to bottom): 48.2°F (9°C), 42.8°F (6°C), 37.4°F (3°C), 32°F (0°C), 26.6°F (-3°C), 21.2°F (-6°C), 15.8°F (-9°C), 10.4°F (-12°C), 5°F (-15°C)

(Months): JAN, FEB, MAR, APRIL, MAY, JUNE, JULY, AUG, SEPT, OCT, NOV, DEC

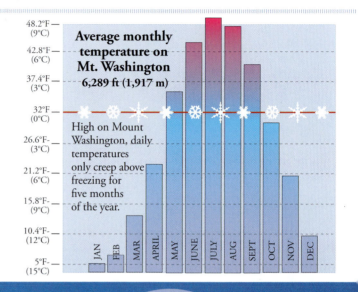

The gray and white color of the snowcock helps it hide among rocks and snow.

The Himalayas are the world's tallest mountains, rising to Mount Everest at 29,016 ft (8,844 m). Nothing lives above about 20,000 ft (6,000 m), where there is permanent snow and ice.

Keeping low is the secret to survival in the mountains. Many plants grow in short cushionlike tufts. The icy wind blows over the tops of these, leaving the stalks and leaves untouched. Small animals hide in burrows or under rocks. Large animals move to find shelter and places to feed.

Himalayan poppies grow 13,000 ft (4,000 m) above sea level in the mountains of Nepal and China. Although the flowers die at the end of summer, their roots stay alive under the soil. The blanket of snow protects the roots from winter ice, so they can sprout again in spring.

CLIFF SCRAMBLERS

North American bighorn sheep have cushionlike pads on their feet so they can jump from rock to rock. Excellent eyesight helps them spot an enemy up to half a mile (1 km) away.

As you travel up a mountain, the average temperature falls by about 1°F for every 300 ft (1°C for every 150 m) you climb. It gets windier the higher you go, and there is more snow and ice. Fewer living things can cope with this increasingly harsh weather, so there are different—and fewer—plants and animals living high up.

Caribou (reindeer)

Dwarf mountain pine

Alpine argus butterfly

Apollo butterfly

Bell heather

Saxifrage

LOW FORESTS
Trees grow in valleys, but cannot cope with the cold and wind higher on the mountain. Caribou live on the edges of the forests.

MONTANE SCRUB
Some trees and shrubs can grow a little way above the forest. They have low, twisted shapes and are called montane scrub.

MOUNTAIN HEATH
Above a height called the scrubline, no trees can grow. Here different heathers are the main plants. A few insects visit their flowers.

ICY TOPS
On the highest tops, snow and ice take over completely. In pockets where snow melts in summer, tough mountain flowers briefly appear.

Among the highest-flying birds are bar-headed geese, which migrate over Mount Everest.

SNOW BLOSSOMS
In early spring, snowbells grow under the snow. They heat the snow and melt tiny spaces around themselves. When the snow melts, they are already in flower.

TINY MOUNTAINEER
Insects avoid the Sun by hiding in holes or under leaves. The world's most abundant insects—springtails—live in all habitats including 20,000 ft (6,000 m) up mountains.

HIGH LIVING
This chubby relative of the hare is called a Mount Everest pika. It makes its home 20,100 ft (6,125 m) up in the Himalayas. That's higher than any other mammal.

FLOWER SHOW
The glacial buttercup is Europe's highest-living flowering plant. It has been seen in flower 14,026 ft (4,275 m) up in the Swiss Alps. It often grows close to glaciers.

the *shrinking* mountain

Climate change is generally making *temperatures rise.* Although it is **difficult to be certain,** scientists think world temperatures in 2100 could be up to *11.5°F (6.4°C) higher* than they are today. That means mountain **plants** and **animals** would have to **move higher** to find the *climate* they need, and to escape from *lowland species* moving in to their home from the lower slopes.

Mountain habitats are shrinking as

Melting the ice
The world has been getting warmer since the end of the last Ice Age around 11,000 years ago. But now greenhouse gases are changing temperatures more quickly. As a result, some glaciers in the Himalayas are shrinking by 100–130 ft (30–40 m) a year.

Disappearing glacier
Since the Glacier National Park was set up in Montana in 1910, glaciers have melted so much that today they only cover a quarter of the area they once occupied. If they go on melting, it could be No-glacier National Park by 2030!

Rocky future
The rock hyrax lives in rocky places throughout Africa. One kind lives 11,500–15,500 ft (3,500–4,700 m) up on Mount Kenya. Eagles are its main enemy there. If the climate gets warmer, it might gain a new hunter as leopards move up the mountain.

As temperatures rise, animals and plants can move up the mountain. In the Himalayas, bharal sheep and yak will be able to move upward, although there will be less space as they go higher. But the chiru antelope on the highest peaks might simply run out of mountain.

The living zones on the mountain for bharal, yak, and chiru antelope will shift with changing climate.

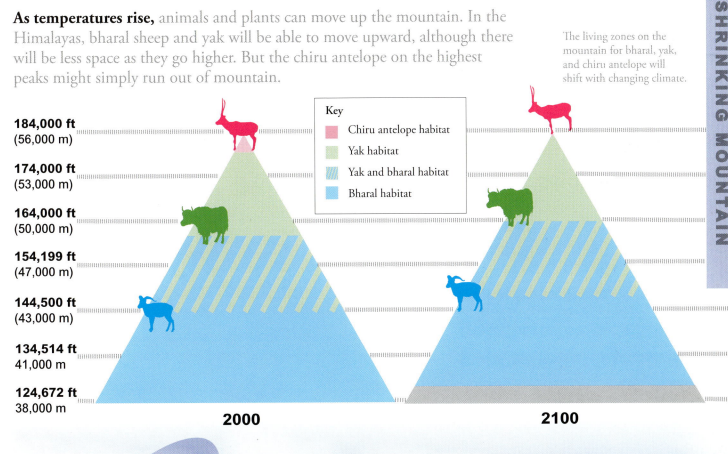

Key
- Chiru antelope habitat
- Yak habitat
- Yak and bharal habitat
- Bharal habitat

184,000 ft (56,000 m)
174,000 ft (53,000 m)
164,000 ft (50,000 m)
154,199 ft (47,000 m)
144,500 ft (43,000 m)
134,514 ft 41,000 m
124,672 ft 38,000 m

2000   **2100**

global temperatures continue to rise.

Snowless bunting
Snow buntings breed high in the Scottish mountains, above 2,900 ft (900 m). A 5°F (3°C) increase in temperature would force their habitat up to 4,440 ft (1,350 m). But there are no mountains that high in the UK, so there would be no place left for the buntings.

Pygmy-possum problem
The tiny mountain pygmy-possum lives up to 7,200 ft (2,200 m) in the mountains of southeast Australia. In winter it hibernates in a burrow under the snow. A slight temperature rise could cut snow cover, leaving it with nowhere to hibernate.

Bad timing
In the Rocky Mountains, the two-lobe larkspur is pollinated by hummingbirds. Warmer weather would make the larkspur flower early. As hummingbirds only visit the mountain on long summer days, they might arrive too late to pollinate the flowers.

the snow leopard

ALTHOUGH AN ENDANGERED ANIMAL, THE SNOW LEOPARD IS STILL HUNTED BY HUMANS

The snow leopard is known for its pale, spotted fur, which helps it hide on its snowy hillside home. The animal is prized by hunters—its fur is used to make expensive coats and rugs, and its bones are used in Chinese medicine. Snow leopards were never common because few other animals live in these high mountains, so food is scarce. Now there may be only 2,500 adults left in a home range three times the size of France.

Snow leopards live in the mountains of central Asia. They are mostly found above the forest zone, and go as high as 20,000 ft (6,000 m) in the Himalayas.

The snow leopard is 2 ft (60 cm) from shoulder to ground.

On the bare hillsides, snow leopards hunt wild sheep, deer, and pikas, as well as goats, like the markhor. The markhor lives in herds of up to 35 animals. Both males and females have large corkscrew-shaped horns.

Markhor

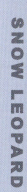

highland ecosystem

Highlands are flat, or gently sloping, upland areas. They are lower than mountains, but like mountains, are very cold in winter. Some animals visit these highlands only in summer, when the Sun bakes down and warms them. However, a few, tough animals live there all year round. The Altiplano is a highland area in the Andes mountains, South America. It is a vast, high-level plain, lying 12,000 ft (3,600 m) above sea level.

On the Altiplano, the mountain viscacha survives extreme temperature changes—from a warm daytime 68°F (20°C), to a freezing -4°F (-20°C) at night.

Culpeo foxes cross the Altiplano plains at night. They creep out onto the salt lakes to hunt for flamingo eggs and chicks.

Flamingos feed on the millions of shrimps that live in the salty water. Pigments in the algae shrimps eat give the flamingos their pink color.

High-level salt lakes 10,000 years ago, a huge lake covered the Altiplano. It has gradually dried out, leaving behind smaller lakes. No rivers run out of these lakes—they simply dry up in the Sun. Salt washed in from rocks makes their water very salty.

High plateau The Drakensburg Plateau in South Africa was raised up as one block of land by earth movements 200 million years ago. It looks like a massive castle, 800 miles (1,290 km) long and rising to 11,420 ft (3,482 m).

Altiplano food chain Tough grasses and spiny shrubs are the commonest plants on the Altiplano. They are difficult for animals to eat and do not provide much goodness, but they form the base of the entire food chain for the area.

Yareta

Ichu grass

Chinchilla

Mara

Puna hawk

Andean condor

PRODUCERS
The rounded, cushionlike yareta bush can survive cold, dry conditions. Ichu is a tough grass found nowhere else in the world.

PRIMARY CONSUMERS
Maras are long-legged relatives of rats. Chinchillas live in South American mountains and highlands. Both animals eat any plants they can find.

SECONDARY CONSUMER
Maras and chinchillas are tempting food for hunters like the puna hawk. In fact, maras and their relatives, called cavies, make up a fifth of the hawk's food.

TOP PREDATOR
The Andean condor is a giant vulture whose wings reach 10 ft (3 m) from tip to tip. It feeds mainly on dead animals, but can kill using its powerful beak.

Very little rain or snow falls on the Altiplano. Most plants here are desert species, such as this cactus.

Vicuñas are wild relatives of llamas. Their fine wool keeps them warm on cold nights.

JEWEL IN THE CLOUD
The slopes of the Drakensberg are often hidden in cloud, so they get lots of rain. Some flowers, including this Drakensberg agapanthus, thrive in the wet climate.

FRENCH TOPS
The Massif Central in France is a flat highland area, reaching 6,187 ft (1,886 m) above sea level. Because it is higher than the surrounding land, it has its own weather and wildlife.

WOOLEN SWEATERS
Few crops can be grown on highland farms because of cold or wet weather, so fields are usually grazed by sheep and cattle, as on this farm in Northumberland, England.

HEATHER EATER
Many upland areas have been changed by humans. In the Scottish Highlands, purple heather is grown to provide food for the red grouse, which people then hunt for sport.

Highlands in danger

There are more people than ever in the world and they all need somewhere to live and work. To fit them in, more *land* is being **used up**, even in many *highland* areas. The city of La Paz, Bolivia, for example, lies in a canyon in the Altiplano. The **city** has now filled the canyon, and a huge suburb called El Alto (the Heights) is spreading onto the highlands above the canyon. El Alto has *taken over* land where wild *plants* and *animals* once lived.

People need houses, so towns have to spread. But we can still make space for wildlife in parks, and provide bird nesting boxes and food in our yards.

In 1900, no one lived in El Alto.

Farming the highland
Life is healthier in the highlands of the Altiplano than on the hot, wet plains below, so many people moved up there to farm. However, farming destroys natural plant cover and places where wild animals live. Also, nearby towns get bigger to supply the farmers.

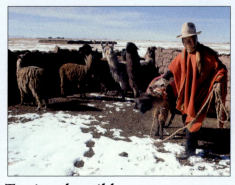

Taming the wild
The best animals to farm on the Altiplano are the ones that belong there naturally. Around 4,000 years ago, people tamed two South American relatives of camels—llamas and alpacas. More than three million of each are now kept on farms there.

Stripping hills
Overgrazing causes problems in highland areas all around the world. Farmers keep as many sheep and cattle as they can on the hillsides. The animals eat all the natural plants. The bare soil and rocks then get washed away in rainstorms.

La Paz city offers work to people from the poorer country areas of Peru and Bolivia. As more of them move to the city, the poor suburb of El Alto spreads rapidly onto land that was once wild highland.

Now 650,000 people live there.

Too many hooves

In Scandinavia, local people herd semiwild caribou for use as food and clothing. By the end of the 1990s, the number of herded caribou had increased to around 750,000. In winter, their many mouths and feet destroy the natural cover of lichens.

Hilltop wind factories

On hilltops, huge turbines use wind to make electricity. Since they do not burn fossil fuels, they help slow climate change. However, windfarms spoil the wild appearance of highlands, and birds flying past are sometimes killed by the giant blades.

Popular place

Three million people a year visit Yellowstone National Park in the Rocky Mountains. There they enjoy the highland scenery and wild animals. But too many people spoil the feeling of wildness and chase away animals. Visitor numbers are now strictly limited.

fragile roof of africa

THE ETHIOPIAN HIGHLANDS ARE AN OUT-OF-THE-WAY HABITAT IN A WAR-TORN REGION OF AFRICA

Few people visit the rocky Ethiopian highlands. As a result many wild animals, like these gelada baboons, still live there. Fossils show the baboons were once much more common in Africa, but they were forced back into the hills as humans took over the lowlands. Their home needs protection—but this is not a high priority in a country troubled by famines, armed rebellions, and war, and where some people are desperately poor.

The Ethiopian Highlands lie in northern Africa. They form a vast dome of high land 600 miles (1,000 km) across and rising to 15,160 ft (4,620 m).

Ethiopian highlands

The gelada baboon's head and body are up to 30 in (76 cm) long.

The walia ibex is a type of mountain goat. Its soft, flexible hooves help it pick its way across rock ledges to nibble grasses and herbs. Although rare, it is still hunted for meat by local people who are short of food.

Charities like Oxfam help Ethiopian people make a living without hunting wild animals. Find out more at www.oxfam.org.uk/coolplanet/kidsweb/world/ethiopia/

mountain valleys

Lauterbrunnen Valley in Berner Oberland, Switzerland

Valleys were formed when ancient rivers cut deep paths through the mountains. They wore away the rock, washing tiny pieces of it—called silt—down to the bottom of the river. Floods spread the silt across the valley floor, creating a rich, fertile soil. Now flowers and trees grow in the soil, sheltered from wind and cold by high valley walls. These plants provide homes and food for animals, birds, and humans.

Food chain The valleys are warmer and more sheltered than the mountaintops and have a richer food chain.

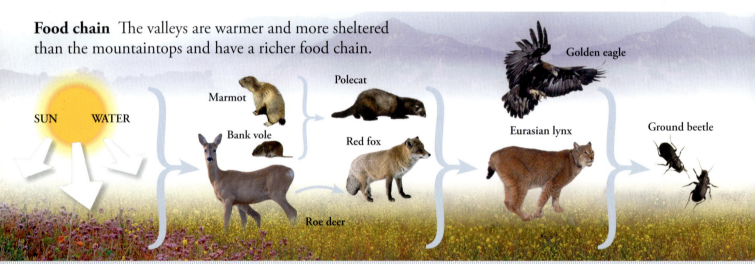

SUN WATER

Marmot

Bank vole

Roe deer

Polecat

Red fox

Golden eagle

Eurasian lynx

Ground beetle

PRODUCERS
Sunshine and regular rain help plants to grow well. These form the base of the valley food chain, providing food for all the animals further up the chain.

PRIMARY CONSUMERS
Marmots are common grazers in mountain areas. Voles, deer, and wild sheep also graze the valley slopes and shelter in the woods.

SECONDARY CONSUMERS
Foxes, polecats, and other small hunters go after marmots, voles, and mice. Foxes kill young roe deer if they get the chance.

TOP CARNIVORES
Although top hunters such as eagles and lynxes prefer to hunt large prey, like deer or wild sheep, they will kill a red fox or a polecat if it crosses their paths.

DECOMPOSERS
Ground beetles are common in mountain valleys. They clean up droppings and the remains of dead animals, helping to put goodness back into the soil.

Return of the Rocky Mountain wolves The last gray wolves in the Rocky Mountains were killed by human hunters about 40 years ago. Wolves keep down numbers of deer, sheep, and goats and stop them from eating all the young trees. In 1995, scientists released 14 wolves back into the Yellowstone National Park. They settled down and began breeding. Today around 250 wolves live in the area.

Mountain valleys Most plants and animals live in the shelter of the valley floor and on the lower slopes. As you climb, it gets colder and windier, so the higher you rise, the fewer species you will find.

SLOPES
High up in the mountains, no trees and shrubs grow because it is too cold. A few tough plants, called alpines, survive to flower in summer, like this gentian. Its roots are a favorite food for voles.

SCRUB
At slightly lower levels, a few trees and shrubs begin to grow. Ice and wind kill off many of their branches, giving them a low and twisted shape. Birds like ptarmigan and bluethroats live there.

WOODS
Below the scrub, trees grow tall since they have more shelter. The level where they start growing, called the treeline, varies with local climate. Woodpeckers feed in the trees, hunted by pine martens (left).

MEADOWS
In summer, meadow flowers bloom on the valley floor and farm animals graze on the rich grass. A blanket of snow protects the meadows through the winter, while insects hibernate in the soil.

RIVERS
Mountain rivers are clean, fresh, and fast-moving. Young insects, called larvae, live among stones on the river bottom. They are food for river birds like the gray wagtail (left) and dipper.

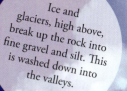

Ice and glaciers, high above, break up the rock into fine gravel and silt. This is washed down into the valleys.

Winds whip over mountain shoulders like this. Few plants live here.

Valley flowers produce nectar to tempt butterflies, including the apollo. In return for this sweet treat, the butterflies pollinate the flowers so seeds can form.

In the Alps and other mountain regions, the displays of valley flowers are among the most colorful you will see anywhere in the world. Grazing by cows and sheep helps keep these areas open and flowery.

mountain valleys

Mountain valleys are great places to visit as tourists. In winter, we can **ski** there. In summer, they offer *walks* or places to go *mountain biking* among beautiful scenery. Tourism provides a **living** for local people. This helps to protect the valleys, because it shows that wild countryside can *bring in money*. But too many people can damage the countryside, and **climate change** might alter the environment for ever.

Lots of people have fun in mountain

Going downhill
People want to enjoy skiing vacations in the mountains, but this means that trees have to be cut down to make ski runs. And when people crowd into skiing areas, wild animals run away. They hide in places where it is difficult for them to live, so they die.

Mountain biking
Mountain walkers leave paths bare, so soil washes away. The tires of mountain bikes do even more harm to paths. Proper bike tracks and good walking trails allow visitors to explore mountain valleys without causing damage.

Modern farming
Old-fashioned farming helps maintain flower-rich meadows. The problem is that mountain farming is hard work and does not pay well, so farms are being bought up, joined together, and farmed with big, modern machines that destroy the meadows.

under threat

Mountain roads The Alps mountain range once stopped people moving between northern Europe and the Mediterranean. But now roads cut through the valleys, including this 119 mile (192 km) route south from Salzburg, Austria.

More and more cars In the early 1970s, 600,000 vehicles a year drove through the Brenner Pass in the Alps. In 1999, 6.5 million cars and trucks drove along this route. The road blocks the movement of wild animals, and traffic fumes damage forests and plants.

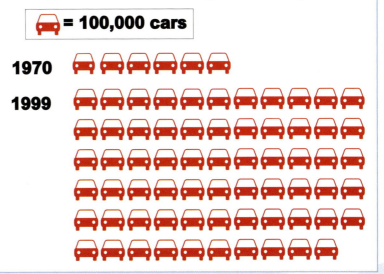

 = 100,000 cars

1970

1999

valleys, but they're easily damaged.

Flooding the lowlands
Scientists are worried that climate change will increase rain and snow fall in some areas. More snow and warmer winters might cause more avalanches. In spring, snow will melt quickly, rushing down rivers and causing floods in the flat plains below.

1979   2002

Shrinking glaciers
Although a few glaciers are still growing (because climate change is making more snow fall on them), most are shrinking in the warmer weather. They are melting faster than ever before. Between 1997 and 2002, the Altsch glacier in the Swiss Alps shrank dramatically.

Wrapping a mountain
This glacier, above the Swiss ski resort of Andermatt, is melting. If it disappears, the local ski industry will suffer and people will lose their jobs, so the local government wrapped it in plastic foam during the summer to try and stop it from melting away.

MAKING A DIFFERENCE

MOUNTAINS NEED OUR HELP!

Mountains around the world are protected as national parks and nature reserves—but some are protected in name only. They are marked on maps, but little is done to keep them safe.

Who's helping?

International organizations are helping local people make a living today, while caring for the environment to help people in the future. The United Nations works for a safe and peaceful future for people worldwide. The World Conservation Union is trying to do the same for plants and animals. It is trying to:

- **teach people** just how important mountains are for our future
- **celebrate** mountains, the wildlife, and people who live there
- develop **new ways of farming** that respect the land and keep it safe
- **protect** mountain habitats and wildlife

People who live in mountains and highlands know how important these areas are. Visit www.mountainvoices.org and find out what they have to say.

Mother and child from the Ethiopian highlands.

what you can do
Find out about charities that help to protect wild mountain areas, or rare wildlife like the snow leopard (right). Search the internet using words such as "mountain" and "conservation."

Mountains are incredibly useful—they provide more than half our freshwater, as well as lumber and minerals, and their rivers make electricity.

what you can do

Every year "International Mountain Day" is on December 11. Why not do a class project on mountains next December? Visit www.fao.org/mnts/intl_mountain_day_en.asp

As the climate changes, butterflies are on the move. Help to record where they live now at www.butterfly-conservation.org

TAKE A MOUNTAIN VACATION

Tourism helps to support the economies of mountain areas. If local people know that it is scenery and wildlife that attract people there, then they will try harder to look after them. By taking a vacation in the mountains, you are playing your part in helping them.

VISIT A RESERVE

When you are in the mountains, try to visit any nature reserves that are open to the public. If lots of people go to them, it is much easier to argue that they should be looked after—and, anyway, they're great places to visit!

SUPPORT THE MOUNTAINS!

KEEP YOUR EYES OPEN

If you do go walking in mountain areas, watch where you are going! Make sure you keep to the paths so you don't damage plants or disturb wildlife that

is not used to visitors. Only ride a mountain bike on routes that are specially marked for mountain bikers.

FRESHWATER

A frog dives into cool, freshwater, a *scarce* resource. Without it neither we nor the world's wildlife can survive.

FRESHWATER

Still, clear water looks soft and inviting, but rushing water is powerful enough to carve out deep canyons and caves. Hidden beneath the surface of almost every body of water—large or small, still or rough—live many different animals and plants. Only the most polluted waters have no life at all.

where on earth...?

Freshwater is in short supply on Earth. Most is hidden away underground as groundwater or locked up in ice. What we see in rivers, lakes, and wetlands is less than one per cent of the total. That tiny amount is vital to us and to Earth's wildlife.

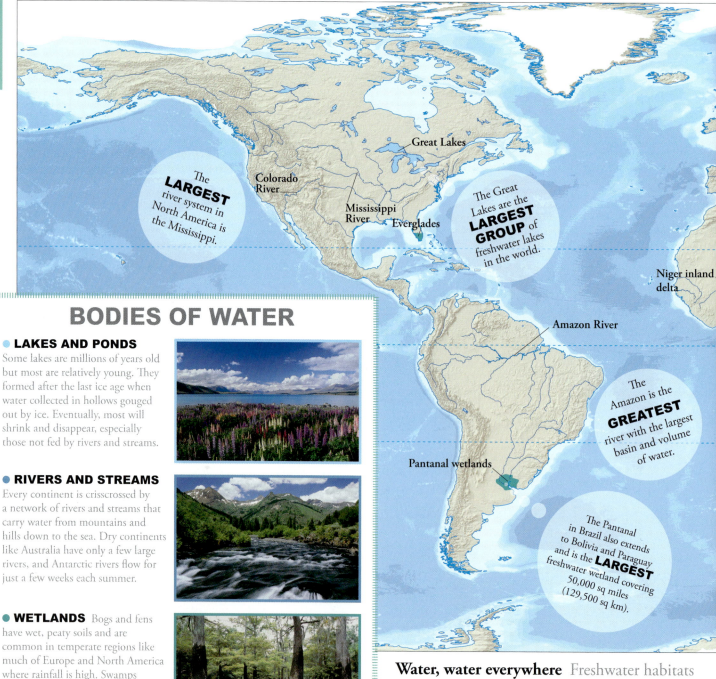

The **LARGEST** river system in North America is the Mississippi.

Great Lakes

Colorado River

Mississippi River

Everglades

The Great Lakes are the **LARGEST GROUP** of freshwater lakes in the world.

Niger inland delta

Amazon River

The Amazon is the **GREATEST** river with the largest basin and volume of water.

Pantanal wetlands

The Pantanal in Brazil also extends to Bolivia and Paraguay and is the **LARGEST** freshwater wetland covering 50,000 sq miles (129,500 sq km).

BODIES OF WATER

● **LAKES AND PONDS**
Some lakes are millions of years old but most are relatively young. They formed after the last ice age when water collected in hollows gouged out by ice. Eventually, most will shrink and disappear, especially those not fed by rivers and streams.

● **RIVERS AND STREAMS**
Every continent is crisscrossed by a network of rivers and streams that carry water from mountains and hills down to the sea. Dry continents like Australia have only a few large rivers, and Antarctic rivers flow for just a few weeks each summer.

● **WETLANDS** Bogs and fens have wet, peaty soils and are common in temperate regions like much of Europe and North America where rainfall is high. Swamps (wetland forests) are common in the tropics, while marshes (wet grasslands) are found worldwide.

Water, water everywhere Freshwater habitats occur all over the world. There are even freshwater springs under the sea along the coast! Exactly what occurs where depends on geology and climate, especially rainfall.

GLACIERS

Glaciers hold nearly three-quarters of the world's freshwater. They form when layers of snow fall in the same place. As they pile up, they turn into a lump of ice. Some glaciers end up in lakes where they slowly melt, adding more water to the lake.

HARDNESS

When it falls, rainwater is almost pure, but streams and rivers absorb minerals as they flow over and through the ground. Rivers in chalky areas pick up calcium and are said to have hard water. Rivers flowing over granite or peat have soft water.

NUTRIENTS

Mountain rivers and lakes are cold and contain little nitrogen and phosphorus so not much can grow in them. But too many nutrients from sewage or farm runoff can cause problems too. A healthy ecosystem needs the right balance of nutrients.

TEMPERATURE

The temperature of rivers and lakes depends on the climate, the depth, and the flow of water. Many rivers in or near the Arctic Circle freeze over during the winter. Some rivers and lakes in hot climates dry up and disappear in summer.

OXYGEN

A rushing bubbling stream picks up a lot more oxygen than a still lake. Stormy waves on large lakes also help to mix up the water and oxygenate it, but in summer deep lake bottoms can become stagnant and animals must move out or die.

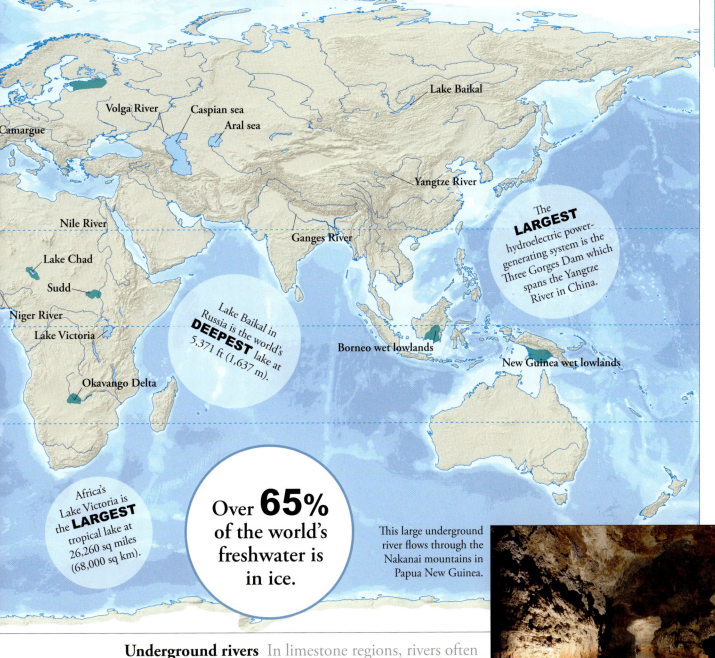

Camargue

Volga River

Caspian sea

Aral sea

Lake Baikal

Nile River

Lake Chad

Sudd

Niger River

Lake Victoria

Okavango Delta

Ganges River

Yangtze River

Borneo wet lowlands

New Guinea wet lowlands

The **LARGEST** hydroelectric power-generating system is the Three Gorges Dam which spans the Yangtze River in China.

Lake Baikal in Russia is the world's **DEEPEST** lake at 5,371 ft (1,637 m).

Africa's Lake Victoria is the **LARGEST** tropical lake at 26,260 sq miles (68,000 sq km).

Over **65%** of the world's freshwater is in ice.

This large underground river flows through the Nakanai mountains in Papua New Guinea.

Underground rivers In limestone regions, rivers often flow underground, disappearing in one place and reappearing in another. They flow through caves and passages formed over time as the limestone is slowly dissolved by slightly acidic water.

rivers **and** streams

Much of our landscape as we know it today was shaped by rivers. The source (beginning) of a river may be a small spring, a lake, or melting ice. As the water flows downhill it collects into small rivulets in cracks and gullies. These merge together forming streams and eventually rivers. A river system with its many tributaries distributes water to a wide area giving life to plants, animals, and people.

The natural winding course of this river in Kenya provides space for a wide variety of wildlife.

1 MELTING ICE
Melting ice and snow provide the starting point for many rivers. Meltwater is also important for sweeping away silt that has built up in rocky canyons.

The water in streams and rivers comes originally from rain and snow. Rainfall upstream affects river flow downstream.

3 DELTAS
Huge amounts of river silt are carried downstream, building up fertile land in large deltas.

2 RIVERS AND STREAMS
Many small streams collect surface water from a wide area called a drainage basin. Then they join up to make bigger rivers.

4 UNDERGROUND RIVERS
Some rivers in limestone areas disappear underground to flow through caves and tunnels, then surface again farther down.

Water that seeps down into the ground is called groundwater. Many wetlands rely on it.

Changing shape Rivers in lowland areas meander or curve across flatter ground. The water on the outside of a bend usually flows faster, cutting away the bank. Water on the inside of a bend flows slowly and drops its load of silt. That's how each curve gets bigger with time.

An oxbow lake is formed when the two ends of a river loop join and the loop gets pinched off.

today

10 years

50 years

ecosystem

River flow The flow of a river changes along its length, and this affects both its landscape and wildlife. Fast water wears down rocks and is a challenging place to live. Slow water drops silt, but is full of nutrients.

WATER SCULPTURE

Over millions of years, the Colorado River has cut down through layers of colorful rocks to form more than 1,000 miles (1,600 km) of canyons, including the Grand Canyon.

RIVER'S END

The Ganges, like most rivers, finishes its journey slowly through a wide delta. The river divides into a network of channels—like the veins in a hand—as it flows into the Bay of Bengal.

RIVER HUNTERS

Giant water lilies in Amazon backwaters provide stepping-stones for the jacana, or lily trotter, as it probes for water insects. Predators lurk both above and below the slow-flowing, murky water.

ALONG THE EDGE

River banks appear and disappear with the water flow rather like ocean shores with the tide. When the water is low, Amazonian butterflies suck up vital minerals from the mud. Other animals come to hunt and drink.

IN THE FAST LANE

Brown bears enjoy a feast of salmon as the fish fling themselves up waterfalls to reach the gravelly headwaters where they lay their eggs. Tumbling water provides these energetic fish with plenty of oxygen.

Tumbling waterfalls help streams and rivers to pick up vital oxygen from the air, but creatures living here must cling on tightly.

Fire salamanders live in damp woods near streams in the mountains of central and southern Europe.

Insect larvae make tasty snacks for fish so caddisfly larvae build a protective home of twigs, stones, and shells.

Dippers are skilled underwater hunters. They plunge into fast streams, clinging to rocks with their strong claws, while searching for insect larvae and water snails. In large pools they use their wings to swim under water.

threatened rivers

There are very few natural rivers left in the world. The flow and **course** of most rivers have been altered by dams and engineering works, which provide water and stop flooding. Changing or **polluting** one part of a river can affect wildlife and people living many miles downstream. Some rivers, such as London's Thames River, have been successfully cleaned up.

Just 21 out of 177 of the world's longest rivers

Damming rivers China's Three Gorges dam across the Yangtze River is one of the world's largest dams. It was built to prevent flooding and to generate clean, renewable hydroelectric power. Above the dam, small streams are now deep rivers and many people have lost their homes.

Polluted rivers Many rivers around the world are polluted with sewage, industrial waste, and farm runoff. In some stretches of India's Ganges River fish and other wildlife are dying due to low oxygen levels, and the water is dirty enough to make swimming dangerous.

Muddied rivers Silt carried by rivers is important for building up fertile floodplains and deltas downstream. But too much silt smothers plants and makes it difficult for fish and birds to hunt. Here, soil washes into the Amazon River as a result of rain forest trees being cut down.

Abstraction in the Nile River Ten countries depend on water from the 4,160 miles (6,700 km) of the world's longest river. The White Nile and Blue Nile branches flow through Uganda, Ethiopia, Sudan, and Egypt, and the river basin also drains water from Tanzania, Burundi, Rwanda, Republic of Congo, Kenya, and Eritrea. The river flow reduces along its route, as water is taken out (abstracted) by each country.

Egypt Egypt is the largest user of Nile water, mainly for crop irrigation. International agreements help to make sure upstream countries allow enough Nile water to reach Egypt. But higher evaporation due to climate change and greater use of water by other developing Nile-basin countries will reduce the flow and may cause further conflict.

Other countries By 2025, the population of all the Nile-basin countries is expected to be double what it was in 1995. Each country will need more water so less will be left for wildlife and people in each downstream country.

Sudan The White Nile and Blue Nile join at Khartoum in Sudan. Much of Sudan is desert but by building irrigation dams, Sudan grows cotton for export, a vital source of revenue.

Nile

White Nile

Blue Nile

Uganda The Nile River begins at the northern end of Lake Victoria in Uganda. Many other streams and rivers from surrounding countries flow into the lake.

Ethiopia The Blue Nile provides much of the water used by Sudan and Egypt in the summer. Seasonal rainfall in the Ethiopian highlands feeds into Lake Tana, the source of this major Nile tributary.

still flow freely from source to sea.

Alien invasion Coypu are dog-sized rodents from South Africa. A few escaped from fur farms in East Anglia, UK, in around 1929 and invaded nearby rivers and fens. They damaged river banks and destroyed reed beds for 50 years before they were finally exterminated.

Natural flood plains Rivers flow along channels they have carved out, but spill over onto natural flood plains after heavy rain. New Orleans, built on a low-lying flood plain, suffered terrible flooding when its flood defenses gave way during Hurricane Katrina in 2005.

Household impact Many cleaning products contain hard-to-break-down chemicals called phosphates. These find their way into rivers, causing a great deal of damage.

Encourage your parents to shop for ecologically friendly cleaning products with no phosphates.

the european beaver

CONSERVATIONISTS ATTEMPT TO RETURN BEAVERS TO THEIR NATURAL HABITAT AFTER DECADES OF EXTINCTION IN THE WILD

Beaver releases In recent years, beaver pairs have been released into three enclosed areas in Scotland, Kent, and Gloucestershire, in the UK. They have electronic tags in their ears and cannot escape. If they breed successfully, and plans are approved, they might once again be seen swimming in rivers and lakes.

Scotland

If trials succeed, Scotland may be the next European country to reintroduce beavers into the wild.

Top hat

Top hats made from beaver skin came into fashion in Europe and America in the 1780s.

Only a few hundred years ago you might have met a beaver, or even a wolf, walking through the wilds of Scotland. Today, though, there are no wild beavers—or wolves—in the whole of Great Britain. Beavers were once common in Europe, but were hunted for their wonderful, soft, waterproof fur. In Great Britain, the last beaver was killed in the 16th century. Now many European countries that once had beavers have brought them back and they are breeding successfully in the wild. European beavers are smaller and less destructive than American beavers, which are the national animal of Canada. They do cut down small trees, but by building dams across streams the beavers create ponds where wetland wildlife can flourish.

lakes and ponds

Lakes and ponds are bodies of still, freshwater that are home to a huge variety of wildlife. Millions of people also rely on lakes for drinking water, fishing, and fun. They vary in size from the immense Lake Superior in North America to tiny pools. Small ponds and lakes in lowland areas are often muddy and full of nutrients from the surrounding land. Some fish survive in stagnant water by gulping air into special air sacs.

A spring-fed pool in the Kruger National Park, South Africa, draws animals in to drink, wallow, and hunt.

Mallard and other wildfowl feed and rest on lakes and ponds. They build nests around the edges hidden among reeds and other plants. On urban ponds they can become quite tame.

Lakes change shape over time. When edge plants die they build up the soil so plants can grow farther out.

Don't release any pet fish, turtles, or terrapins into the wild where they can upset the fragile ecosystem.

LAKE BAIKAL

Lake Baikal in the heart of Siberia, Russia, at 5,371 ft (1,637m) deep, is the deepest lake in the world. It also holds around a fifth of the Earth's surface freshwater.

Special seals Baikal seals are unique in living permanently in freshwater. They are endemic (unique) to Lake Baikal and cannot be found anywhere else. Nearly half the fish in Lake Baikal are also endemic. The number of seals is going down because people hunt them for their meat and fur. Disease and pollution add to their problems.

ecosystem

SUN

OSPREYS
Ospreys hunt over lakes, snatching up pike and other fish.

Osprey

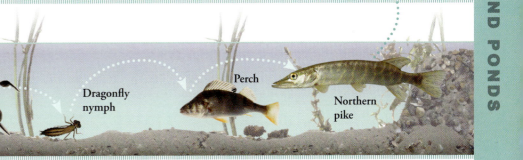

Pondweed

Tadpoles

Dragonfly nymph

Perch

Northern pike

PLANT LIFE
Submerged plants grow lushly in shallow, well-lit water where they form the basis of the food chain. Plant plankton also provide food.

AMPHIBIANS
Young tadpoles graze on soft plant material and debris and, when older, eat injured tadpoles and other animals. Adult newts eat tadpoles.

POND NYMPHS
Many types of insects, including dragonfly nymphs, eat tadpoles. These predators hunt underwater for years then change into flying adults.

COARSE FISH
Young perch feed on tiny plankton animals and later grow fat on insect larvae. As they get bigger they eat other small fish, sometimes even their own young.

TOP PREDATORS
Pike are experts at stalking perch and other fish. They have hundreds of small teeth and can also snap up frogs, voles, and even ducklings.

Lake Tekapo, high in the mountains of New Zealand, is filled by cold, clean water from rain and melting snow.

Beneath the surface, plants cover the lake bed and help to oxygenate the water. They grow deep down in clear water.

STILL LIFE
Pond snails living in stagnant water have no gills. Instead, they come to the surface and breathe air using a simple lung. They also absorb oxygen from the water through their skin.

SALT LAKES
Salt Lake in Utah is saltier than the sea! Water with mineral salts flows in but not out of the lake, and the sun evaporates the water. In winter the lake freezes as shown here.

HERE TODAY, GONE TOMORROW
Fairy shrimps appear as if by magic in temporary pools. They hatch from tiny eggs that are so tough they can survive for years in dried out mud.

LAKE TITICACA
The Peruvian Uros people live on Lake Titicaca 13,000 ft (4,000 m) above sea level. They build their homes on floating islands and fish from boats crafted entirely from reeds.

losing lakes

Many towns and cities around the world have **grown** up around lakes, which provide a ready *supply* of water and food, especially *fish*. Taking **too much** water out of the lakes for **industry** and farming, and putting too much **waste** back in affects both people and wildlife. Climate change can cause lakes to shrink or *dry up* if there is less rainfall. Shrinking lakes can also become more salty as minerals in the water are *concentrated*.

Reducing water use in homes, industry,

Water sports Lakes are great places for vacation activities. Lake Geneva in Switzerland used to be very polluted from nearby industrial cities. Tourists complained and eventually the lake was cleaned up. But sewage from tourist boats and hotels can still pollute lakes.

Choked up 19th-century travelers to Brazil admired the lovely water hyacinth and took plants back to grow at home. Some escaped into the wild. Now in Africa many lakes are choked by this fast-growing invader.

Fishing problems Many people live around the shores of Lake Malawi in Africa. They take water and fish to eat from the lake. But as the human population goes up, they need more fish, so fish numbers are going down. Birds that feed on fish are also becoming scarce.

1989 **2003**

Disappearing lake Fifty years ago, the Aral sea, an immense inland salt lake in central Asia, was full of life. Since then it has shrunk, slowly at first but increasingly quickly. Water that should flow into the lake from two mighty rivers has been taken away to water cotton fields in Uzbekistan. It takes more than 700 gallons (2,700 liters) of water to grow enough cotton for one T-shirt.

More than 60,000 people were once employed in the Aral fishing industry. Now fish have gone and fishing boats lie stranded.

and agriculture will help wildlife.

Water vole Water voles are one of Britain's most endangered mammals because many of the lake edges and streams where they live have disappeared. But now "Ratty," as Kenneth Grahame called the water vole in his book *The Wind in the Willows,* is finding space along man-made canals.

New for old Millions of tons of gravel are used every year to make cement for the building industry. Digging it out of the ground leaves huge empty holes, but if these pits are landscaped and allowed to fill with water, they can make wonderful new wildlife sites for water birds.

Moving to town In some places, toads and frogs are now more common in urban areas than on farmland. In the past, villages and farms often had ponds. Many natural ponds have disappeared, but now people in towns are creating garden ponds and welcoming back wildlife.

the dragonfly

DRAGONFLIES ARE BEAUTIFUL AND ALSO USEFUL. THEY EAT MANY PEST INSECTS, BUT CANNOT LIVE IN POLLUTED WATER

Dragonflies are a beautiful sight, skimming over lakes and ponds almost anywhere in the world. These magnificent flying creatures need clean water and plenty of prey both above and below water. So a good population of dragonflies patroling tirelessly around a lake indicates that it is healthy and unpolluted. They are excellent at catching pests, too. Sadly, over the past 40 years, numbers have gone down and three British dragonfly species have become extinct through habitat loss. However, climate change is bringing new species, and wildlife groups are busy digging new ponds to attract dragonflies.

Metamorphosis
Dragonfly eggs hatch into sinister-looking nymphs. Fierce hunters, they spend several years underwater gobbling up mosquito larvae, worms, and even tadpoles. Once big and fat they molt their skins and develop broad wings.

1 When it is big enough, the dragonfly nymph crawls up a plant stem out of reach of the water.

2 It holds on tightly, the skin across its back splits and it starts to pull itself out of its old skin.

3 Blood soon flows into its two pairs of crumpled wings and once dry, it flies gracefully away.

While some grow to the size of a hand, most adult dragonflies are smaller than your palm. Nymphs are shorter and fatter.

Nymph

Adult

Japanese damselfly Damselflies are closely related to dragonflies but have a slender body and wide-set eyes. In Japan, they are symbols of success, strength, and courage.

swamps **and** bogs

Walking through a swamp or bog is difficult, smelly, and wet! But wetlands, including marshes and fens, are very important habitats for wildlife, especially birds. All depend on a good supply of water from rain, runoff, and river floods. Climate change, flood defenses, and drainage can cut off this supply. The constant flow of water washes nutrients away, so wetland plants grow slowly but often live a long time.

The Marsh Arabs of Iraq build floating houses from reeds. They fish, grow rice, and raise buffalo. Much of their marshland has been drained.

At night, alligators hunt through flooded cypress forests for turtles and fish.

There are rich pickings for wading birds and plenty of insects as long as water levels remain high.

Swamp life Most trees die if flooded by water, but cypress forests in southern North America are adapted to wet conditions. Their wide trunks flare out at the base to support them and their cones float away to disperse their seeds. These forests are home to manatees, snakes, alligators, and many birds.

Bog moss Continuous cold rain and mist is just right for bog-moss, or sphagnum, the main plant in northern hemisphere bogs. Sphagnum has no roots but the stems soak up water like a sponge. The stem tips grow while the lower parts die off and form a soggy mat.

BLANKET BOG
In the Scottish Highlands huge areas are covered in a thick blanket of peat bog up to 23 ft (7 m) deep that has built up over thousands of years from the remains of bog-moss.

ecosystem

In the past, wetland areas provided a living for local people. They caught fish, shot wildfowl, dug peat for fuel, and cut reeds.

Wetland use Today, wetland areas are more likely to be used for walking, sailing, and watching wildlife, but reeds are still cut for thatching houses.

Eel trap

Binoculars

House made of reeds

Duck

EEL FISHING
Eels are common in wetland pools and waterways. They are caught in special traps and fyke nets. Bait tempts the eels into these tunnel-shaped structures.

RECREATION
Wetlands are excellent for bird watching. In summer, bitterns, harriers, and warblers nest in the tall reeds, while in winter ducks and geese feed in flooded areas.

REEDS FOR THATCHING
Tall, flexible stems of Norfolk reed are ideal for thatching houses. Reeds harvested from wetland nature reserves regrow quickly and help fund conservation work.

WILDFOWL FOR FOOD
In the past, people in wetland areas ate ducks, geese, and even swans. Today, wildfowl are hunted for sport while farmed birds provide us with food.

With their sharp eyesight, egrets stab small fish sheltering between the tree roots.

Upright cypress "knees" grow up from the roots. They help support the tree and bring air to the roots.

BOGGED DOWN
In 1984, peat cutters at a moor in Cheshire, UK, found the remains of 2,000-year-old "Lindow man." He was killed and thrown in a bog, where acidic water preserved him.

CARNIVOROUS PLANTS
Plants living in boggy places can get extra nutrients from insect prey. The leaves of the Venus fly-trap snap shut when a fly lands on them. The prisoner is dissolved and absorbed.

CAMARGUE HORSES
Herds of white horses have lived in the French Camargue for centuries. This vast plain of marshlands, lakes, and reedbeds is one of Europe's most important wetlands.

COASTAL WETLANDS
Tropical-island wetlands are rich in wildlife. The Caroni swamp in Trinidad has freshwater marshes, tidal mangroves, and lagoons where scarlet ibis and howler monkeys live.

Wet and wild areas support a huge variety of wildlife, from birds to frogs.

from wet...

Wetlands are often thought of as wasteland—and many have been drained, transforming them from wild, **wet** areas to tame, rich farmland. Developed countries have begun restoring them

What has happened?

As the world's population increases, more and more land is needed for housing, agriculture, and industry. Wetland areas are drained and dams are built to store water for irrigation and prevent flooding.

Building homes on floodplains and deltas has destroyed many wetlands.

Farming areas of fen and marsh has turned these wetlands into dry land.

The world has lost as much as 50%

Peat cutting Peat compost helps gardeners to keep their soil moist and plants grow well in it. But demand for peat compost has encouraged commercial cutting, and entire peat bogs and their wildlife are being destroyed.

Encourage your parents to buy peat-free compost, which does not contribute to the destruction of wetlands.

Rice cultivation In central California, large areas of wetland have been drained to grow wheat and oats. But now some farmers are growing rice in wet fields. Flooding the fields in the winter after harvest provides a temporary home to migrating ducks and geese.

Wet islands Many formerly huge European wetlands are now only small islands dotted among dry farmland. In the UK, the rare swallowtail butterfly is stranded in the lakes and marshes of the Norfolk Broads. Now there are plans to recreate some larger wetland areas.

...to dry

Once people move in, the water must be drained or contained.

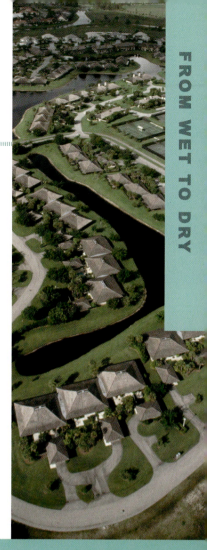

by reflooding drained **farmland**. This can prevent flooding elsewhere, as storm water is soaked up. Also, as in the Florida Everglades, restored wetlands benefit *wildlife* and tourism.

Pollution from homes and industry is spread by rivers and streams.

Dams prevent seasonal floods essential for many wetland areas.

Peat excavation has destroyed bogs that took thousands of years to form.

# of its wetlands in the last 100 years.

Polluted wetlands Important wetlands need a wide buffer zone around them to prevent pollution. In 1998 a mining dam broke in Spain. Millions of tons of toxic waste flooded into nearby rivers and was carried into the Donana nature park, where it killed many fish.

SUMMER   WINTER

Dry to wet In summer, cattle graze, hay is made, and birds nest in the Ouse Washes, UK. In winter, water from rivers on each side is pumped into the area to save farmland from flooding. Thousands of swans, geese, and ducks fly into this seasonal wetland.

Constructed wetlands Large wetlands can purify water, a very useful service. At Show Low in northeastern Arizona, lakes and marshes are the final part of a big natural plan to clean wastewater. The resulting wetland is very attractive to wildlife—a double benefit.

the everglades

MORE THAN HALF THE EVERGLADES WETLANDS HAVE BEEN LOST TO AGRICULTURE AND DEVELOPMENT

Imagine finding an alligator in your swimming pool! That's a problem faced by some residents of Florida. Alligator numbers have grown since hunting ended in 1967, but the human population has risen, too—bad news for the Everglades that cover most of southern Florida. This wet wilderness depends on water flowing from Lake Okeechobee in the north towars the Gulf of Mexico in the south, a flow now interrupted by land drainage for housing, flood prevention, and city water supplies.

The restoration plan for the Everglades (CERP) covers a much wider area than the Everglades themselves.

The Everglades

Tomatoes need a lot of water to grow. In southern Florida, crops are often irrigated with huge amounts of water pumped out of wells. But diverting this well water onto the fields reduces the natural flow of water heading towards the Everglades.

Now an ambitious plan is under way to help both people and wildlife. The Comprehensive Everglades Restoration Plan (CERP) aims to improve the flow of water to the Everglades, provide people and farms with water, and prevent flooding. It will cost billions of dollars and take at least twenty years to complete, but the funding for this ambitious project is already starting to dry up.

MAKING A DIFFERENCE

Who's helping and how

* **Governments** The US's Clean Water Act (1977) set out to stop factories and farms from polluting lakes and rivers. It has been updated and improved ever since.

* **Local governments** Innercity rivers are being cleaned up and restored. London's Thames River is home to salmon and other wildlife once more.

* **Construction companies** Some new houses are built with the technology to recycle "gray" (dirty) water or rainwater so it can be used to flush the toilet.

* **Inventors** Removing the salt from seawater so it can be used for drinking takes a lot of energy, but inventors are finding ways to do this using the power of the Sun instead.

what you can do
Some toads and frogs return to the lake where they were born to mate and lay their eggs. Join a wildlife group that helps these creatures reach their destination safely.

SHOPPING
- Dishwashing liquid *
- Laundry detergent *
- Shower gel *
- Toilet-bowl cleaner *
- Fish for supper
(from sustainable source)
- Boots for community cleanup day

*= eco-friendly

Goodman's
TOMATO SEEDS

Arrange to visit a local nature reserve.

It's not all bad news. Take action in your own home and neighborhood. If everyone did this the Earth would be much healthier.

what you can do
Instead of buying a bottle of water when you're out and about, get into the habit of carrying a reuseable flask or bottle.

TERRIFIC TOILET
Low-flush!
Eco-friendly!

WOW

Uses **1.5 gallons**
(Some toilets use over twice that!)

When you need a new toilet, buy one that uses less water. Meanwhile put a brick in the cistern to save water.

Friends of Lake Local
Pleasantville,
US

Invitation

Dear neighbor,

Let's make Lake Local sparkle!

Please join us on Saturday July 7 at the lakeside.

1 pm Community cleanup
6 pm Barbecue

See you there!

what you can do
Build a pond in your backyard to attract frogs, insects, and plants whose habitats are being destroyed.

PAVE OVER PART OF BACKYARD FOR A PATIO

PROS	CONS
- More space for patio furniture and barbeque - Less lawn to mow	- Lose flower garden and apple tree - Less pretty view from inside - Less play space in the yard - Rain drainage won't be as good with less lawn

Don't do it!

Get some peat-free potting soil to plant seeds.

what you can do
Visit a wetlands nature reserve. You enjoy the wildlife, and your entrance fee will help to protect the creatures and maintain the environment.

4   THE DAILY NEWS

AMAZON SWIMMER
THE WORLD NEEDS CLEAN RIVERS

April 16, 2007

On April 8, 2007, Slovenian marathon swimmer Martin Strel became the first person to swim the entire 4,000 miles (6,400 km) of the Amazon. Of his epic 66-day feat, the swimmer said "My aim was to promote a message of clean rivers, clean water, and friendship, because these rivers and water have to stay clean, otherwise the world will surely collapse. The Amazon River is still very clean, local people use it as a natural resource, and I believe it should stay clean forever."

Water shortage predicted for summer
Scientists working at the Meteorological Office are predicting an unusually dry summer. River levels have already dropped after Spring rains. Secretary of the Interior hinted restrictions on water use were...warned...

OCEANS

The oceans cover **70** percent of our planet. Yet they are the most *mysterious* and unexplored part of it.

OCEANS

For years we have used the ocean as a garbage can and a playground, and seen it as a never-ending source of food. Now, as oceans become warmer and more acidic, they face new problems. Our challenge is to repair some of the damage and make them cleaner and healthier for the future.

where on earth...?

The Ocean is the world's biggest habitat. Five huge oceans fill deep basins between the continents. Smaller seas like the Mediterranean and the Red Sea fill gaps and splits around the edges. Seas and oceans contain 97 percent of the water on Earth.

ARCTIC OCEAN

Earth's outer skin is made up of large tectonic **PLATES**. Earthquakes, volcanoes, and hot water vents occur where ocean plates meet.

ASIA

Arabian Gulf

Red Sea

The Mariana Trench, near Guam in the western North Pacific, is the **DEEPEST** place in the ocean. The bottom of the trench is called the Challenger Deep. Its depth is 36,000 ft (11,000 m).

Mariana Trench

The **SALTIEST** water in the ocean is found in the Arabian Gulf and the Red Sea.

INDIAN OCEAN

AUSTRALIA

Hurricane Katrina, 2005

Ocean and atmosphere The Earth's oceans help to keep the planet warm. They act a bit like a giant hot-water bottle, absorbing heat from the Sun. They also have surface currents that carry warm water from the tropics toward the poles.

DEPTH

The oceans are on average 12,500 ft (3,800 m) deep. Beneath their flat surface lies a hidden landscape. Chains of underwater mountains with vast flat plains on either side are as dramatic as anything on land. The deepest spots are the steep ocean trenches.

SALTINESS

Seawater is far too salty for us to drink. Two pints (1 liter) contains about 1.2 oz (35 g) of salt—a heaped tablespoon. Hot sun causes water to evaporate, which makes some parts even saltier. Melting ice and rivers flowing into the ocean make other parts less salty.

TEMPERATURE

Ocean temperatures vary from about 77–86°F (25–30°C) in tropical parts where it is warm enough to swim all year round, to 32–36°F (0°–2°C) in the Arctic and Southern oceans. Deep ocean water stays at a chilly 36°F (2°C) everywhere.

PRESSURE

Seawater is very heavy and exerts a crushing pressure on everything in the ocean. Water pressure is measured in units called bars and increases by one bar for every 32.8 ft (10 m) depth. Pressure has little effect on animals without air spaces, like fish.

OXYGEN

Oxygen dissolves easily in the ocean as waves and currents stir the water around. Even at the deepest depths there is enough for marine creatures to absorb or breathe through gills.

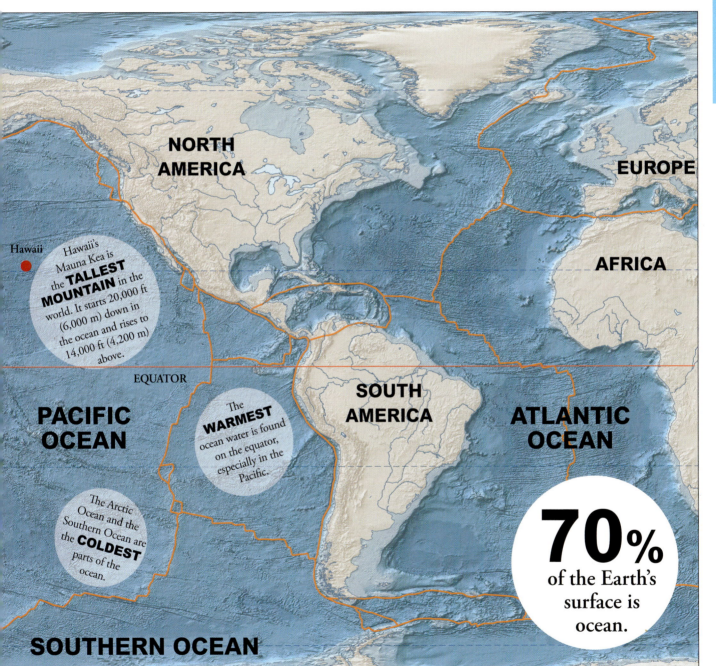

NORTH AMERICA

EUROPE

AFRICA

Hawaii

Hawaii's Mauna Kea is the **TALLEST MOUNTAIN** in the world. It starts 20,000 ft (6,000 m) down in the ocean and rises to 14,000 ft (4,200 m) above.

EQUATOR

SOUTH AMERICA

PACIFIC OCEAN

The **WARMEST** ocean water is found on the equator, especially in the Pacific.

ATLANTIC OCEAN

The Arctic Ocean and the Southern Ocean are the **COLDEST** parts of the ocean.

70%
of the Earth's surface is ocean.

SOUTHERN OCEAN

People living by the sea often have warmer weather in winter and cooler weather in summer than those living farther inland. Oceans also affect the climate—sometimes by creating hurricanes. This happens when the hot summer sun causes water to evaporate from the ocean. This warm, water-laden air rises into the atmosphere. Cooler air rushes in to replace it, which results in strong winds. The winds spin as the Earth turns round on its axis and a hurricane is born.

ocean ecosystem

The ocean is a constantly moving mass of water with movement both on the surface and from the depths to the top. Wind-driven waves stir up the surface and break on the shores. Circulating water carries oxygen and nutrients. Without these, the ocean depths and seabed would be stagnant and dead, but, in fact, the opposite is true: life flourishes throughout the ocean.

DUCK OVERBOARD!
Scientists learned a great deal about ocean currents by tracking thousands of plastic bath toys, accidentally washed overboard from a cargo ship in 1992.

Foaming waves whipped up by strong winds help pull oxygen and carbon dioxide into the water. Oxygen levels are highest near the surface.

THE OCEAN ZONES

0–650 ft (0–200 meters)

650–10,000 ft (200–3,000 meters)

10,000–30,000 ft (3,000–9,000 meters)

Seashore and continental shelf These are the underwater edges of continents. Shelves slope gently, usually for 30–60 miles (50–100 km). This well-lit zone is rich in nutrients and full of plant and animal life. Most commercial fisheries are over continental shelves.

Continental slope Falling steeply downward from the continental shelf, the sloping seabed consists mainly of a thick blanket of sand and mud washed down from the land. Many animals live here, especially in rocky areas, although it is too dark for seaweed to grow.

Abyssal plain Right at the bottom of the continental slope, the seabed flattens out into the abyssal plain. Miles of soft muddy sediments called oozes stretch away across the ocean basins. Deep sea fish, squid, prawns, and jellyfish live in the cold dark water above.

Global conveyor belt

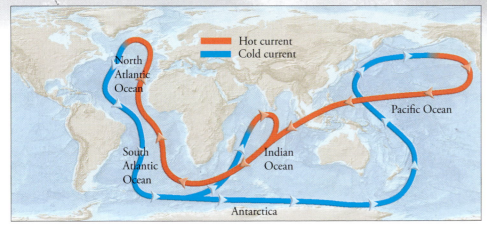

Hot current
Cold current

North Atlantic Ocean

Pacific Ocean

South Atlantic Ocean

Indian Ocean

Antarctica

Water circulates slowly through the ocean like a giant factory conveyor belt. Heavy cold water sinks deep into the North Atlantic and flows south toward Antarctica. It then flows east and north into the Indian and Pacific oceans, then back west into the Atlantic.

A mass of seawater takes 1,000 years to complete a lap.

Seashore sand is formed as the ocean batters rocks and breaks up pebbles, seashells, and corals. The shell remains of tiny plankton drift down to form deep ocean mud.

Gulls pick food from surface waters and along the shore. Other seabirds can dive deep and swim in search of fish.

VERTICAL CURRENTS

When warm and cold ocean currents meet they push water down or up. Upwelling brings nutrients from the seabed to the surface, causing plankton to grow, and producing food for fish and other creatures.

ATLANTIC CONVEYOR

The Atlantic Conveyor is a system of currents that includes the Gulf Stream. It keeps western Europe, including the west coast of Ireland (below), warm by carrying warm water north from the tropics.

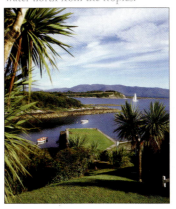

OCEAN FOOD

Life in the ocean is fuelled by floating plant plankton. A complex food web links animals at all depths to the plankton at the surface. Plant plankton makes food using the Sun's energy.

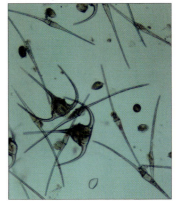

TIDAL CURRENTS

Tides are the regular in and out movements of the ocean from the shore. They are caused by the pulling effect (gravity) of the Moon and Sun. Whirlpools can form when water is pulled through narrow channels.

using the ocean

The way we use the ocean has *changed* over the centuries. More people live on the coast and there is more **industry** there, too. In the developed world, *traditional* fishing has

1950

2005

Snorkeling in the Caribbean is no longer just a dream.

"I do like to be beside the seaside..." Seaside vacations became very popular in Britain after 1938, when workers were first entitled to paid vacations. People visited seaside towns such as Blackpool to stroll along the beach in the bracing air. Now cheap air travel has changed all this.

Sifting cockles from the sand is hard work and takes time.

Harvesting machines can destroy cockle beds if collecting is unrestricted.

Food for free People all over the world have collected wild shellfish since early times. Shellfish were traditionally dug out by hand, with small ones left behind to grow and reproduce. Modern commercial machines dig or suck out huge numbers.

Empty cockle shells

Clipper ships traded goods all over the world in the 19th century.

Modern container ships carry huge amounts of cargo.

Sailing the seas Traveling by sailing ship used to mean months at sea—if disease or pirates didn't get you! But sailing ships used no fuel and wrecks caused little pollution. Today, ships crossing our oceans are almost all fueled by oil. Oil pollution is widespread and shipwrecks can destroy wildlife.

Traditional fishing continues in India.

Modern ships allow fishing far out to sea in deep water.

Hook, line, and sinker Over the past two centuries, fishing methods have changed dramatically. Fishing communities used to catch enough fish to supply their families and local markets. Without fridges the catch could not be sent very far. Today frozen and canned fish can be sent anywhere.

mostly given way to large-scale **commercial** fishing. However, fishing **communities** in some parts of the world still live in *harmony* with the sea, taking only what they need. Where this **balance** has been lost, the ocean is **suffering**. Governments are introducing **regulations** to help, such as laws controlling the amount of untreated sewage that can be released into the sea.

Estuary havens Estuaries——the tidal parts of a river——have always provided shelter and food for wading birds, ducks, and geese. Their rich muddy shores are full of juicy worms and shellfish, and migrating birds use them like highway service stations. Now many large estuaries have developed into industrial ports.

Flocks of gulls and knots are a common sight in estuaries.

This estuary in Barcelona is now an important Spanish port.

Learning from the seashore Seashores provide wonderful outdoor classrooms for the study of marine life. In the 1800s, naturalists wrote about the wonders of the seashore. Many people were inspired to visit the coast, but popular sites were damaged. Now students mostly take photographs.

Drying and preserving seashore animals was a popular Victorian pastime.

Cameras capture the beauty of the seashore without damage.

Ocean exploration It has always been difficult to explore under the ocean. Early diving suits were heavy and clumsy and scientific study of the oceans has lagged far behind that on land. Modern submersibles and ROVs (Remotely Operated Vehicles) can explore and film the deep ocean.

Early divers received air pumped down a tube from the surface.

The French Nautile submersible can reach depths of 20,000 ft (6,000 m).

Riches from the sea Pearls and sponges have been harvested from the sea for centuries. Pearl divers could reach amazing depths with no air supply. Use of modern diving gear has resulted in overcollection of valuable corals and sponges. **Natural sponge**

Few pearl divers remain, as pearl oysters are now farmed.

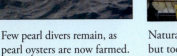
Natural bath sponges are still harvested but today they are rare.

215

coastal ecosystem

The coastal environment is an ever-changing place where the land meets the ocean. Coasts and shores are formed by ocean waves and the geology of the area. Hard granite cliffs can resist the sea and remain unchanged for hundreds of years. However, softer rocks, sand, and mud are easily worn away. Coastal plant communities, such as saltmarshes, help protect the coast by shielding it from the impact of waves and weather.

Battering waves carve dramatic rocky stacks and headlands from coastal cliffs. Here, soft limestone cliffs off southeast Australia have worn away to form 12 tall islands called the Apostles.

Seabirds find rich pickings along the shore. Seaweed cast up by storms contains juicy sand hoppers and worms. Seagulls tackle tough starfish, while herons stab at fish in pools.

Life on the seashore Plants and animals along the water's edge are mainly those that can tolerate salt spray and occasional submergence in the sea. Those farther inland are marine (sea) plants and animals that have adapted to living out of water for a while.

Black-headed gulls are common in the northern hemisphere. They have white heads in winter.

SAND DUNES

Low tides expose vast areas of sand, which the wind whips into small mounds and dips called dunes. Marram grass and other plants bind the dunes so they don't blow away.

The sea's edge It's a tough life surviving between land and sea. Every tide washes in a fresh supply of food, but also brings in oil and garbage. Waves roll pebbles and rocks around crushing animals and plants. Wind and sun dry everything out. Yet shores around the world support an amazing variety of life.

Rockpool oases When the tide is out, rockpools provide a refuge from baking sun or freezing cold. Young fish shelter there safe from large predators, but rain can dilute the pools and sunshine can cause them to evaporate.

Mussels

Bladder wrack

Starfish

Tern

SHELLFISH
Mussels and oysters can survive pounding waves by fixing themselves to rocks using strong threads (byssus) or special glue.

SEAWEED
The slime that makes seaweeds so slippery stops them from drying out and helps them survive out of water.

STARFISH
Hundreds of tiny sucker-feet help starfish to climb over rocks. Starfish also use them to pull apart and eat shellfish.

SEABIRDS
Terns catch fish by plunging into the sea. Other seabirds patrol the beaches at low tide picking out crabs and worms.

Lichens, flowers, and trees cling to skyscraper cliffs. Long roots, thick leaves, and tough skin help keep water in.

Sand, rock, pools, and cliffs provide homes for a wide variety of marine life.

MANGROVE SWAMPS
Most forests will only grow on dry land. Mangroves, however, can tolerate salt and grow along sheltered tropical shores. Their tangled roots stabilize shifting mud and sand.

PEBBLE BEACH
Pebble and shingle beaches and spits build up as strong waves and currents pull stones from deep water and toss them onto the shore. Storms can remove whole beaches just as quickly.

CLIFF LIFE
Steep rocky cliffs provide a home safe from most predators for nesting seabirds, their eggs, and young. With little soil or water, a few plants cling on, storing water in their leaves.

NEW COAST
Most coasts form over millions of years, but sometimes a new coastline appears suddenly. Earthquakes push land up or volcanoes pour lava into the sea. Colonization follows swiftly.

crumbling coast

Stone Age people found plenty of food along the ocean's *shoreline*. Today, over **half** the world's population live near the coast. Millions of tourists also visit these areas. All this *activity* damages mangroves, marshes, sand dunes, and coastal coral reefs—natural defenses against **erosion** and *flooding*. People living in low-lying coastal areas such as the Maldives and Bangladesh are already suffering the effects of **rising** sea levels.

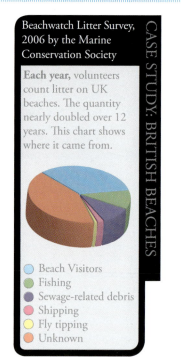

Beachwatch Litter Survey, 2006 by the Marine Conservation Society

Each year, volunteers count litter on UK beaches. The quantity nearly doubled over 12 years. This chart shows where it came from.

- Beach Visitors
- Fishing
- Sewage-related debris
- Shipping
- Fly tipping
- Unknown

This graph is based on information taken from satellites about sea level increases between 1992 and 2004. It shows what could happen to sea levels over the next hundred years if climate change continues at its current rate.

| 1990 | 2000 | 2010 | 2020 | 2030 | 2040 |

Boating blues Ships and boats from dinghies to oil tankers carry people and goods all over the ocean. Pollution is a risk when ships leak or sink offshore. Oil spills kill seabirds and mammals and smother beaches. Cleaning up the mess is expensive.

Sewage Raw or poorly treated sewage is pumped into the sea even in developed countries. Out at sea it fertilizes plant plankton. Closer to shore it is a health hazard to swimmers and surfers. Harmful chemicals from factories can also end up on the shore.

People pressure People in cold northern countries go south in search of sunshine for their vacations. Too many seaside hotels, tourist beaches, and golf courses can destroy important wildlife habitats and tourists may trample on and disturb wildlife.

Coastal cities Many of the world's major cities are near the coast, where rivers flow into the sea. These places were chosen because the rivers made it easy to get out to sea to trade with other countries. Unfortunately, they also make it easy for storm surges and rising sea levels to flood these cities if they are not protected by barriers.

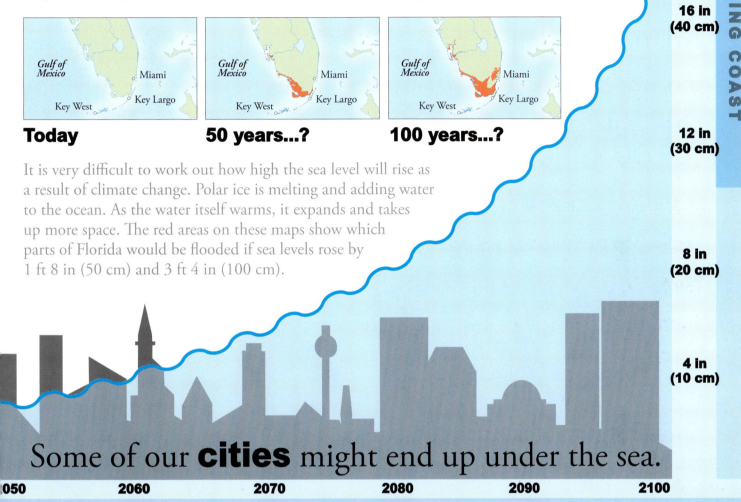

Today

50 years...?

100 years...?

It is very difficult to work out how high the sea level will rise as a result of climate change. Polar ice is melting and adding water to the ocean. As the water itself warms, it expands and takes up more space. The red areas on these maps show which parts of Florida would be flooded if sea levels rose by 1 ft 8 in (50 cm) and 3 ft 4 in (100 cm).

20 in (50 cm)

16 in (40 cm)

12 in (30 cm)

8 in (20 cm)

4 in (10 cm)

Some of our **cities** might end up under the sea.

050   2060   2070   2080   2090   2100

Storm sculpture Over the centuries, coastlines and seashores gradually wear away or build up. This house in California looks set to fall into the Pacific. Violent storms can change a beach overnight, and climate change may bring more intense storms.

Stealing from the sea To increase their living space, the people of Singapore moved their coastline outward, reclaiming land from the sea. Some coral reefs have been destroyed and the once clear waters have become murky.

Mangrove farming About half the world's mangrove forests have been destroyed in the last 50 years, mostly to create ponds for prawn and shrimp farms. Villages without mangroves are more likely to be swamped by storms and tsunamis.

Turtles don't live on beaches, but they visit regularly.

turtle VS

ALL SEVEN SPECIES OF MARINE TURTLE FACE EXTINCTION TODAY. HUMANS POSE THE GREATEST

Although they spend their lives at sea, turtles begin life on land. Take the green sea turtle in Hawaii. An adult female mates at sea once every two to eight years. She finds the beach where she was born, crawls ashore, and digs a hole in the sand

THE CASE FOR TURTLES...

Turtles are already struggling to survive—as few as one in 1,000 babies reaches adulthood. They do not start to breed until they are between 10 and 50 years old, so even with protection it could take many years before numbers start to recover. Turtles need quiet and darkness to lay their eggs. They can't nest when there are people on the beach. The newly hatched babies rely on moonlight reflecting off water to guide them into the ocean so hotel lights send them in the wrong direction. Tourists are bad news for turtles.

Goods made of turtle shell may not be brought into the UK and US, but poachers still catch and kill turtles to make souvenirs for tourists. Hundreds of turtle shell ashtrays, hairclips, ornaments, and musical instruments have been seized by UK and US customs.

In some countries it is now illegal to catch turtles for their meat or to collect turtle eggs, yet both are still being caught and eaten in some parts of the world.

Some fisherman fit hatches called TEDs (turtle exclusion devices) to their fishing nets so turtles can escape.

Take all your litter home after a visit to the beach, particularly plastic bags that turtles might mistake for food.

Divers and snorkelers can frighten turtles by holding onto them under water.

tourist

THREAT, AND ALSO OFFER THE BEST CHANCE OF SURVIVAL TO THESE CREATURES

Tourists love to visit beaches, but sometimes they don't make very good guests.

where she lays around 100 eggs. She leaves, but may return several times to lay more eggs. Later the eggs hatch. The baby turtles scrabble out of the nest and dash to the sea. They swim off quickly to keep from being eaten by crabs, fish, and birds.

THE CASE FOR TOURISTS...

Tourists are becoming interested in, and concerned for, the wildlife of the places they visit. Local people who once collected turtle eggs to sell as food now guide tourists who wish to see nesting turtles. Tourist centers buy eggs from local collectors and then hatch and rear them, eventually releasing them into the wild. Watching their release is becoming a great tourist attraction. Tourists also help local police return turtles rescued from poachers to the sea. Turtle farms have a part to play in conservation. They are a tourist attraction and they provide meat for local markets. Tourism might be just the thing that saves turtles.

Tourists bring much-needed money to many beautiful but poor parts of the world. The beaches of Bali and Mexico, for example, if properly looked after, can sustain wildlife while also providing a good living to local people through tourism.

Some beaches ask tourists to stay away at night so as not to disturb nesting turtles.

TURTLE FACTS

The Hawksbill turtle is the source of traditional "tortoise shell." Its carapace (shell) is marbled with amber, yellow, or brown.

The Leatherback turtle is one of the largest living reptiles. The biggest ever recorded was nearly 10 ft (3 m) from nose to tail and weighed 2,020 lbs (916 kg).

Kemp's Ridley turtles are the most endangered of all. They nest in broad daylight along only one small stretch of coastline in the Gulf of Mexico.

The temperature of a turtle's nest determines the sex of the young. Turtles are thought to dig their nests to different depths to affect the temperature.

seabed ecosystem

The ocean seabed varies from hard rock to soft sediment. At the edges of the land, it is a patchwork of rock, sand, and mud, where vast numbers of sea creatures live. It is here that most of the world's fishing is done. Water current, water temperature, the depth, and type of seabed—these all affect what plants and animals live where.

Volcanic springs, called hydrothermal vents, erupt from the ocean floor. Chemicals in the water nourish bacteria, which are themselves eaten by creatures living on the ocean floor.

Shrimps and prawns crawl over the seabed.

Kelp forests are home to a wide variety of fish and invertebrates. Orange garibaldi fish live in Californian kelp forests.

SHALLOW SEDIMENTS
Much shallow seabed is covered in mud and sand. Valuable scallops lie in shallow depressions hiding from starfish. Buried shellfish take in water using siphons like drinking straws.

NO PLACE LIKE HOME
Sponges, sea squirts, and similar animals form underwater jungles on rocky seabeds. They do not need to move to find food. Ocean currents bring drifting plankton to them.

NEW BEGINNINGS
Fixed animals such as sponges cannot move to find a mate, so they produce tiny larvae that drift and then settle on bare rocks. This shipwreck has become covered in marine life.

STEALTHY PREDATORS
Colorful sea slugs and other mobile predators graze the kelp forests in the same way that limpets and sea urchins graze seaweeds. Their bright colors warn of their horrid taste.

Kelp

Kelp uses
This family of seaweeds has many uses and is harvested from the wild on a commercial scale. Although the holdfast (base of the plant) is left behind to regrow, some animals lose their home and supply of food when the seaweed is cut.

Sushi

Alginates in ice cream

Shampoo

Petri dish growing bacteria in agar

Kelp tablets

SUSHI
Sushi is a Japanese food of rice and raw fish often rolled up in sheets of *nori* (laver), a valuable red seaweed grown in ocean farms.

ALGINATES
If you like ice cream then you like eating seaweed! Kelp and seaweeds contain sticky alginates and gums, which are used in its manufacture.

COSMETICS
Seaweed extracts have been used in cosmetics since Roman times and today are found in shampoo, shaving cream, and skin lotions.

AGAR
Agar is made from harvested red seaweeds. It is a valuable jellylike substance that is used to grow bacteria in medicine and research.

SUPPLEMENTS
Seaweeds contain many minerals and vitamins and can be taken in tablets to promote health. Seaweed is also widely eaten as food by people and animals.

Like underwater rabbits, sea urchins graze the seaweed undergrowth down to a short turf. Sea otters and large fish eat sea urchins.

Harbour seals hunt through the forest for fish, slipping easily between the kelp stipes (stems).

BLUE HOLES
In some places the ocean extends under the land. Dry cave systems in the Bahamas flooded when the sea level rose thousands of years ago. They are now home to rare animals.

Flattened rays blend in with the seabed.

Kelp forests
These cover the rocky seabed in shallow water around temperate and cold coasts. Off Pacific North America these giant brown seaweeds grow to 165 ft (50 m). Smaller ones grow around Europe and in the Arctic Circle.

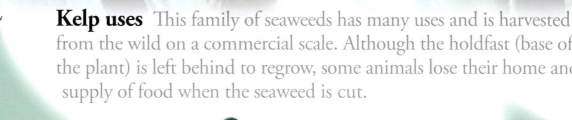

seabed destruction

Fishing boats around the world **drag** heavy nets across the seabed to catch fish, shellfish, and shrimps. They **plow up** the seabed and also catch a lot of *unwanted* animals. Fishermen use special **nets** and try to avoid fish-breeding areas to minimize the **damage**, but trawling is still very *destructive*. In the North Sea, the seabed is *scoured* many times every year. This heavy-duty fishing damages the homes of the **animals** the fish feed on, resulting in *fewer* fish.

Trawling is incredibly destructive...

... but the extent of the damage is largely hidden from view.

Mountain fisheries Huge shoals of fish and squid circle the tops of seamounts—extinct volcanoes rising thousands of yards from the seabed. Fishing fleets are destroying these unique and remote places. We need to protect them now!

Deep-sea dumping The shallow ocean seabed has been used as a dumping ground for many centuries. However, a recent proposal to dump an old oil rig in the deep ocean caused a public outcry. In the depths things only decay very slowly.

Mining the oceans Each year, thousands of tons of sand and gravel seabed are removed for use in the construction industry. Areas must be chosen carefully because it takes at least 10 years of protection for a mined area to get back to normal.

Scooping up Trawlers vary in size from small inshore boats to huge ships that can stay at sea for weeks. The biggest trawl nets can be 200 ft (60 m) across.

The nets are hauled back in using a special frame and strong winches.

Slow-growing sea fans, sponges, and other animals were destroyed when trawlers fished over rocky reefs in Lyme Bay, UK. Although it was legal to fish there, fishermen had earlier agreed not to.

Repeated trawling reduces the biodiversity (number of species and habitats) in an area.

Some trawlers have nets that can hop over low rocks without tearing. Now even more areas can be trawled.

Trawling is the most destructive legal fishing method used today.

Heavy otter boards guide the net over the seabed and keep it open.

Urchin plagues Plagues of sea urchins can destroy California giant kelp forests by munching through seaweed stems so that the plants break off. There are too many urchins because the large sheephead fish that eat them have been overfished.

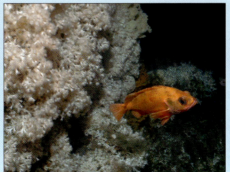

***Lophelia* reef** As shallow fisheries run out of fish, trawlers are targeting fish living in deep water. In the North Atlantic, the trawls are destroying delicate reefs of sponges and cold-water corals called *Lophelia*, some of which are thousands of years old.

Unsorted catch As a trawl net is hauled in, it comes up with all sorts of unwanted animals as well as the target fish. Most of this by-catch is thrown back overboard. Using different-sized nets can help to prevent this.

coral reef ecosystem

Coral reefs can be found in the warm, clear water of the tropics. Each reef is formed by many different corals growing packed together. Every coral is a colony of tiny animals called polyps, and every polyp builds a hard limestone cup around itself. The polyps divide, adding new polyps with their own cups on top of the old ones, and over time the reef expands. Tiny algae live inside the polyps, sharing the food they make in return for a safe home. Reefs also house clams, sponges, and seaweeds.

A fringing coral reef surrounds this island with a colorful halo. The corals grow in the shallow water where there is a hard seabed they can fasten onto.

Giant anemones provide a safe home to crabs, prawns, and clownfish, which are immune to their stings.

Sharks are top predators and help keep reefs healthy by killing weak and sick fish.

A riot of color Life is crowded and colorful on a coral reef. Hundreds of species of fish swim around, through, between, and under the coral. In the dense crowds, fish use bright colors and patterns to find a mate, recognize enemies, confuse predators, and camouflage themselves.

Barrel sponges grow large enough to fit a person inside. They grow slowly and live for many years.

CORAL
Corals come in many shapes and sizes. Each colony develops from a tiny larva hatched from a floating egg. The corals grow upward and outward, facing toward the Sun.

Underwater rain forest A healthy coral reef bursts with life just as a tropical rain forest does. Hundreds of species of coral provide homes and food for fish, crabs, starfish, sea urchins, and shells. The creatures depend on one another. If one link in this food chain is removed, many other species may also disappear. Destroying the coral is like cutting down forest trees.

Essential reefs
Local people round the world depend on coral reefs for food and for their living. Reefs also support a huge tourist industry worldwide.

Lobster

Prawns

Giant clam

Natural sponge

Medicine

Waterproof camera

Mask and snorkel

Beach huts

SEAFOOD
Coral reefs provide about 10 percent of the world harvest of fish and shellfish. That's vital protein for people living near them.

MEDICINES
Scientists are developing the chemicals used by sponges and other reef animals to ward off predators into drugs to treat cancer and arthritis.

TOURISM
Undamaged coral reefs with abundant fish populations attract many tourists. Tourism provides local people with money and jobs.

PROTECTION
Coral reefs form a barrier to waves and protect shorelines from erosion. They can lessen damage to coastal villages from huge waves called tsunamis.

If you visit a coral reef, make sure you don't disturb any of the wildlife, or damage the reef itself.

At night many fish rest safely hidden beneath coral tables and between coral branches.

SPONGES
Many small reef animals find shelter inside hollow sponges, but only turtles and sea slugs relish eating them. The bright colors of sponges warn enemies that they taste dreadful!

SEA SLUGS
Sharks are not the only predators on the reef. Sea slugs hunt, too. They munch holes in anemones, soft corals, sponges, and other fixed animal colonies that cannot escape.

FISH
The reef provides shelter, a place to live, and food for hundreds of fish. Some graze on seaweeds, others eat the coral itself, hunt for worms and crabs in the reef, or stalk other fish.

SEAGRASS
Seagrasses grow in shallow sandy areas, often near to coral reefs. Unlike corals, they root themselves in the shifting seabed. Sea cows (dugongs) and turtles graze these lush meadows.

dying coral

Reefs throughout the Indian Ocean were badly **damaged** in 1998 when sea surface temperatures *rose* to the highest recorded levels in 150 years. In some areas, up to 90 percent of the corals bleached (got rid of the colorful algae that normally live with them) and died. Dead coral is soon smothered in algae and animals and breaks up. The unusual **weather pattern** that caused this is called *El Niño*. It is happening more often, possibly due to global ***climate change***. Although the coral is slowly growing back, many reefs will be permanently destroyed if regular bleaching takes place.

Governments worldwide need to

A room with a view Hotels and beach houses built at the edge of the sea cause erosion when trees binding the soil together are cut down. Sewage and silt then drift out and smother reefs. Rising tourist numbers mean more hotels and houses, but careful planning can help.

Diver's paradise Coral is easily broken by feet and divers' fins. Some popular reefs in the Red Sea have been nearly destroyed by dive boats dropping their anchors on them. Permanent mooring buoys are part of the solution, as is raising awareness of the issues among tourists.

White out When corals are stressed—for example, when water temperature increases—they expel the tiny algae that live in their tissues. Without the colored algae the corals appear white or bleached. The algae return if the stress is taken away, but otherwise the corals die.

Disappearing reefs Already at least 11 percent of the world's coral reefs have been completely destroyed, and a further 16 percent are badly damaged. Scientists predict that even more will die. Damaged corals will regrow once the pressure is taken off them, but the variety of coral is often lost.

BRAIN
Often, damaged brain corals never recover. They can be several yards across, but take hundreds of years to grow to this size.

STAGHORN
Thickets of staghorn coral grow in the shallows. They are delicate structures, easily broken by divers' fins and boat anchors.

MUSHROOM
Mushroom corals thrive on damaged reefs and can cope with silty water. They can turn themselves the right way up again if upturned.

TABLE
Tables of *Acropora* coral are easily broken by storms and the bombs fishermen sometimes use. But they also grow back quickly.

LEAF
Some leafy corals look like chips, others like cabbages, but all provide important hideaways for small reef animals.

Scientists drill into coral and carefully extract a core.

Like trees, corals have annual growth rings and can live for hundreds of years. They respond to changes in temperature and water clarity by growing at different rates. Scientists can use coral cores to form a record of changing conditions in the ocean.

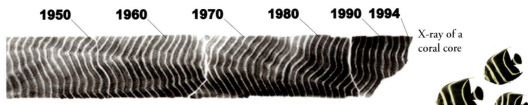

1950 1960 1970 1980 1990 1994

X-ray of a coral core

work together to save our reefs.

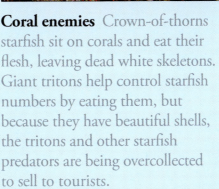

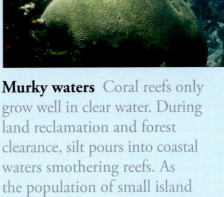

Bombs away In Malaysia, Indonesia, and the Philippines reef fish stocks have declined through overfishing. Some fishermen have illegally resorted to throwing homemade bombs onto reefs to kill and stun fish. The bombs destroy the reef so fish stocks decline even further.

Coral enemies Crown-of-thorns starfish sit on corals and eat their flesh, leaving dead white skeletons. Giant tritons help control starfish numbers by eating them, but because they have beautiful shells, the tritons and other starfish predators are being overcollected to sell to tourists.

Murky waters Coral reefs only grow well in clear water. During land reclamation and forest clearance, silt pours into coastal waters smothering reefs. As the population of small island countries grows, houses, runways, and roads are built and more reefs struggle to survive.

the open

The open waters of an ocean, there are no solid surfaces. Nothing stays still so there is nothing for animals to hide behind or under (except maybe one another). They can't pin their prey to the bottom to eat it because the seabed is so far down. Animals either drift with the current or are strong swimmers. Some have bizarre shapes that help them to float, while hunters such as tuna, sharks, and dolphins are streamlined for fast swimming. Some fish, like sardines, live in huge shoals that protect them from predators, but also make them more vulnerable to modern fishing techniques, which can detect and catch whole shoals. Plant plankton floats in the sunlit surface waters. At night, animals rise up to feed on plankton and each other.

In US waters, ship collisions kill about 10 whales each year. To avoid this, ships must keep to a strict speed limit in whale habitats.

The ocean makes up over 90 percent of the planet's living space, but much of it is dark and cold with little food available. Some areas of open ocean are like deserts with only a few animals.

There are no fences in the water, but the oceans do have borders. Different countries own parts of the seas.

Who owns the ocean? Most countries with a coastline have signed up to the *Law of the Sea* Treaty. This sets boundaries and gives nations exclusive rights to their waters. Territorial waters extend 12 nautical miles (nm) offshore, and an Exclusive Economic Zone (EEZ) extends 200 nm. Ocean areas beyond EEZs are International.

OUTSIZED ANIMALS
The largest animal on Earth, the blue whale, roams the open ocean. Whales can grow to huge sizes because salt water is dense and supports their heavy bodies.

Roaming free Most open-ocean animals spend their lives in the same general area, but a few are true ocean wanderers. Leatherback turtles travel the oceans in search of jellyfish. Humpback whales migrate each fall from cold, food-rich waters to the tropics where they breed. International agreements are needed to protect such animals.

ocean ecosystem

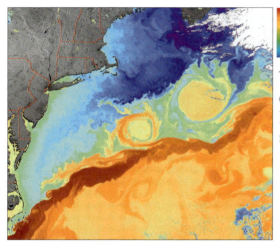

Red color shows warmest water, purple shows coldest.

Walls in the sea Invisible barriers keep floating plankton and fish in their own particular areas and depths. These barriers are ocean fronts and eddies, where water currents of different temperatures and saltiness meet. Here, two warm-water eddies have swirled away into nearby cold water, carrying plankton and fish with them.

Satellites record the surface temperature and amount of plant plankton in ocean water by measuring electromagnetic radiation. Computers convert the data into colored pictures.

Open water is a dangerous place for seals when white sharks are around. These fearsome predators roam worldwide in the ocean.

LIGHTS ON
Deepsea fish drift in permanent darkness. But many produce their own bioluminescent light. Light patterns help them catch prey, find mates, and avoid enemies.

LIGHTS OUT
The rainbow colors of light, especially reds, disappear a short distance below the surface. This deep-sea red jellyfish always looks black so it is hidden in dim light.

HUGE SHOALS
Out in the open ocean there is nowhere to hide. Living in huge shoals helps protect fish like these sardines from predators, but makes it easier for fishing boats to catch them.

DIVING DEEP
Elephant seals can hold their breath for up to two hours and dive to 5,000 ft (1,500 m) deep to search for food. Humans need pressure-proof submersibles to dive this deep.

threatened ocean

Out at sea, far away from land, the human impact on the ocean can still be felt. Many of the **threats** are invisible, like changes in water *quality* and chemistry. Even the normal flow of ocean currents may be changing as water *temperatures* increase through global warming. Other effects are more obvious. Great drifts of **litter** collect where ocean **currents** meet. Wandering leatherback turtles die out at sea after eating plastic bags or "balloon race" balloons. As they rest, flocks of seabirds drift into *oily washings* from ships' fuel tanks.

Some of the greatest and most damaging

El Niño Every few years, the cold current flowing north along the west coast of South America is diverted by a strong easterly flow of warm water from the central Pacific Ocean. The new balance between warm and cold currents, called *El Niño* alters the weather, affecting fishing. Climate change may bring more *El Niños*.

Tourist troubles Watching or snorkeling with whales and whale sharks can be an amazing experience. These animals' value to tourism is a good reason for conservation. However, too much human contact can disturb migration and feeding patterns, so good tour operators follow accepted codes of conduct.

Not so silent ocean Whales and dolphins find their way around under water by making high pitched noises and then listening for echoes that bounce back, much as bats do on land. Loud noises from earthquake research, naval exercises, and ships can confuse them, and sometimes whole groups get stranded on the shore and die.

The **International Whaling Commission** (IWC) was set up in 1946 to protect the great whales. The 78 member nations agree how many and which whales can be killed each year.

Adopt a whale through a wildlife charity. You'll receive information and photos so you can learn more about whales.

FOR

● Japan catches hundreds of great whales each year, providing vital data for conservation and management of whale stocks. Sending meat to the market helps pay for this research.

● In the Faeroe Islands, the annual "grind"—slaughter of pilot whales—is a traditional, and not a commercial, fishing activity carried out by native people.

● Whale stocks have recovered enough to allow some commercial whaling again. The scientific program should lead to more sustainable whaling in the future.

● All of the Southern Ocean (and part of the Indian Ocean) is a whale sanctuary.

The GREAT WHALE debate...

Is there any reason not to hunt whales for food? Does their intelligence and importance in the ocean ecosystem make it unethical to kill them?

● Over four million people a year go on whale-watching trips. Live whales are becoming more valuable than dead ones. Whale watching is educational and fun and has created many jobs.

● There are few whales left. Their numbers have still not recovered from overfishing in the 1800s. Many die each year from boat collisions, stranding, and pollution.

AGAINST

● "Scientific whaling" is an excuse to sell whale meat to Japanese supermarkets. There is no need to kill hundreds of whales for data. A few would do. Unscrupulous sailors from Korea, Norway, and Japan also kill whales illegally and sell the meat.

● Scientists can study living whales. Many can be recognized from photographs of their tail markings, skin and blubber can be taken for DNA analysis, and movements can be recorded with satellite tags. These supply enough data for management.

● All the products that are, or used to be, made from whales such as oil, soap, glue, leather, and lubricants can now be made synthetically or obtained from other sources.

threats to the ocean are invisible.

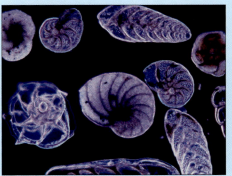

Ocean acidification The ocean absorbs huge amounts of carbon dioxide from the atmosphere. It enables plankton, many bacteria, and seaweed to grow, but burning fossil fuels results in more carbon dioxide entering the ocean and making it more acidic. This could dissolve the shells of plant plankton and other animals.

Alien species Animals and plants moved by mistake from one ocean to another can become serious pests. In the Mediterranean, a green seaweed has spread over large areas and is killing seabed animals by smothering them. It probably escaped from an aquarium near Monaco and floated away in ocean currents.

Red tides Sometimes whole areas of ocean turn red when tiny colored plankton plants called *dinoflagellates* multiply very rapidly. As they grow, they produce poisons that can kill fish and make people ill. Red tides occur naturally but the nutrients from sewage can make them worse.

shark finning

SHARKS ARE IMPORTANT TOP PREDATORS IN THE OCEAN. REMOVING THEM IS VERY DAMAGING.

DROWNING SHARK

This Gray Reef shark has been caught, finned, and thrown back onto a reef in Thailand. Sharks grow slowly and give birth to just a few live young after many months of pregnancy. If too many sharks are taken, numbers decline quickly because they cannot breed fast enough to replace those caught.

Don't eat shark-fin soup, and tell your friends and family about shark finning so this harmful practice can be stopped.

Blue shark

The blue shark is the most heavily fished shark in the world.

In Hong Kong and China, shark-fin soup is traditionally served at weddings and special occasions. As these countries have become richer, demand for the soup has increased.

Shark fins hung out to dry

Shark fins are rather tasteless, so pork and chicken are used to give shark-fin soup flavor. Fibers from the fins make the soup glutinous (gooey).

Shark-fin soup

Shark finning is a very wasteful type of fishing in which the sharks' fins are cut off and kept while their bodies are thrown back into the sea. Most shark finning takes place on large ships far out at sea when the boats are out fishing for fish such as tuna. Sometimes the sharks are killed before the fins are removed, but often they are thrown back overboard still alive because shark meat does not make much money for the fishermen and the refrigerator space on the boat is needed for more valuable fish. Sharks' fins are one of the most valuable fish products in the world, along with caviar. The number of sharks in the ocean today is a fraction of what it was a few years ago. Some Atlantic shark populations have gone down by 80 percent in the last 15 years.

Who caught all the fish?

Fishing has undergone a revolution in the last 50 years. Today enormous factory ships roam the seas, equipped with fish-finding sonar and processing systems that include freezing and canning equipment. Dragging enormous nets behind them,

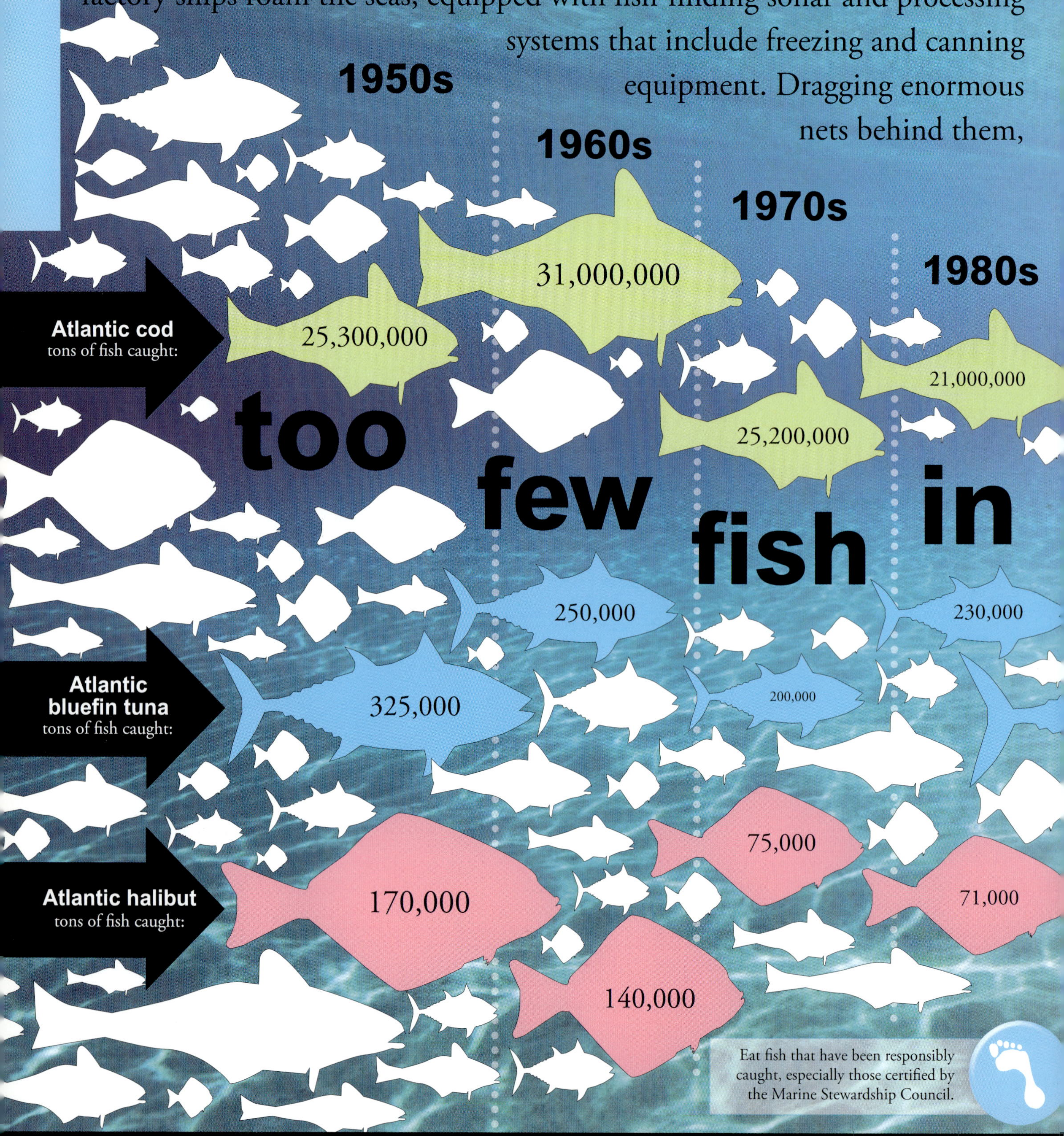

1950s

1960s

1970s

1980s

Atlantic cod
tons of fish caught:

25,300,000

31,000,000

25,200,000

21,000,000

too few fish in

Atlantic bluefin tuna
tons of fish caught:

325,000

250,000

200,000

230,000

Atlantic halibut
tons of fish caught:

170,000

140,000

75,000

71,000

Eat fish that have been responsibly caught, especially those certified by the Marine Stewardship Council.

: are

We did.

they scoop up almost everything in their path, including many unwanted creatures, called by-catch. Most countries regulate fishing, sometimes quite well. But overfishing means there are already far fewer fish left for us to catch.

THE STORY OF COD

Cod is a wonderful fish. Nutritious and tasty, it is enjoyed by people throughout the northern hemisphere. Cod live in great shoals and one large female can lay several million eggs each year. Early European explorers claimed that there were so many cod, they could catch them by dropping baskets into the water. Everyone thought the supply would never run out. But modern fishing is so efficient that cod stocks are now collapsing.

Atlantic cod

Cod used to be one of the most abundant fish in the North Atlantic and has always been the favorite fish in "fish and chips." Now, in the North Sea, cod stocks are so low that for the last five years experts have recommended a total cod-fishing ban. But still the fishing goes on.

1990s

12,700,000

2000s
till now

5,400,000

2010s?

2020s?

GOING, GOING, GONE...?

the sea

400,000

216,000

30,000

50,000

HALIBUT AND TUNA

The amount of halibut caught has been going down since the 1960s as their numbers have dwindled. Blue-fin tuna catches have gone up since the 1970s but in the past two years the catch has plummeted. This is because continuous overfishing has removed too many adult breeding fish so now too few young are produced.

"Dolphin-friendly" tuna come from boats that use very long fishing lines with baited hooks. This saves dolphins from being caught in tuna nets. But the bait also attracts albatrosses, and thousands are pulled underwater and drown.

throw

MAKING A DIFFERENCE

Look out for shark egg cases

Scientists want help to find out more about sharks. Don't worry, there's no danger involved!

Shark egg case

Simply visit your local beach and if you find any egg cases pick them up and take them home. Check out the website below for more info.

www.eggcase.org

Help find my egg cases!

DOLPHIN ADOPTION

ADOPT A DOLPHIN ADOPT A DOLPHIN ADOPT

This is to certify that

Charlie Duffy
....
(Name here)

is recognized by the Dolphin adoption agency as an official protector of

Smiley the Dolphin
....
(Name here)

what you can do

Adopt a dolphin! With this program, you get a cuddly dolphin, certificate, and updates on the dolphin's progress: www.donation4charity.org/wwf-adopt-a-dolphin.php

Dear Congressperson

Please can the government create more marine nature reserves in the US? These provide an important safe haven for fish, birds, and other seaside creatures from activities that are damaging—like trawling the seafloor or building on coastal land. Even dog walking can upset nesting birds.

If the reserves include visitor's centers, people could go and learn about the sea and its ecology. The more people value what is beneath the waves, the more life there will flourish.

I look forward to hear

what you can do

Don't buy marine souvenirs (shells, starfish, sponges, even dried out puffer fish). If there is no market, the fish won't be killed.

YOUR CONGRESSPERSON
CAPITOL HILL
WASHINGTON, D.C.

8 THE DAILY NEWS   February 20, 2007

HARNESSING THE OCEAN'S POWER

SCOTLAND TO GET MASSIVE "WAVE FARM"

The world's biggest wave energy farm is to be created off the coast of Orkney in Scotland. The Pelamis device has been tested at the European Marine Energy Centre (Emec) on Orkney by Leith-based company Ocean Power Delivery. Scottish Power wants to commission four more at the same site. Deputy First Minister Nicol Stephen announced a £13m ($26 m) funding package that will also allow a number of other marine energy devices to be tested. Ocean Power Delivery has already exported the Pelamis for use in a commercial wave farm. Now Scottish Power is planning a venture which it believes could create enough power for 2,000 homes.

...rges battered the coast of England ...bad weather

If you love the sea, you can learn more about the creatures living in and near it, and what you can do to help protect them.

PLASTIKI IN THE PACIFIC

David de Rothschild is setting sail in his plastic boat, the *Plastiki*, for the Great Pacific Garbage Patch—to "document an ocean of trash, on a boat made of trash".

Garbage floating in the sea

This area of the Pacific is a mass of floating plastic pieces caught in a swirling current. It is the size of Texas and 300 ft (90 m) deep, weighing an estimated 3 million tons.

Most plastic doesn't biodegrade; it just turns into smaller and smaller pieces until it is the size of dust. Fish and birds mistake the plastic debris for food, and filter-feeders such as jellyfish ingest the tiny particles. The area is a death-trap for marine life.

Plastic is cheap. We use it briefly and then throw it away. But it doesn't really go away. Lots of it ends up in the sea...

what you can do
Talk "trash" with friends and family and spread the word about the Garbage Patch. Pick up litter at the beach, and recycle plastic.

White Island, New Zealand

See this website to find out more:
http://science.howstuffworks.com/great-pacific-garbage-patch.htm

HELPING

THE EARTH

The Earth is one huge ecosystem in which everything is **connected** under one atmosphere. How we live in our **small patch** of the planet affects everything, everywhere.

HELPING THE EARTH

living with change

Records show that the world has been getting warmer for the last 100 years. People need to adapt to the changing climate, to **heavier** storms, or in some places, much *less* rain.

A tornado and lightning hit a field in the Midwest.

The weather is becoming more extreme.

In the future water may be more precious than oil.

Drought Sub-Saharan Africa, already a poor area, is likely to suffer even worse droughts as a result of climate change. An international agreement called the Kyoto Protocol means that poor countries like those in Africa can get money from rich countries by selling "carbon credits." Carbon credits can be earned by planting trees, or using renewable energy.

Desertification is creating millions of eco-refugees.

Hurricanes Warmer seas are already leading to stronger tropical storms. Hurricane Katrina, which hit the US in 2005, was one of the most devastating hurricanes ever recorded. Much of the damage was due to failure of the city's flood defenses. These are now being rebuilt, stronger and higher than ever, and countries all over the world are reassessing their defenses.

Hurricane Katrina swirling over the coast of Louisiana.

Altering the atmosphere Over the last 600,000 years, the amount of carbon dioxide (CO_2) in the atmosphere has affected the average temperature on Earth. By burning fossil fuels, humans are sending extra CO_2 into the atmosphere and temperatures are rising.

The obvious answer to halting this worrying trend is to reduce emissions of greenhouse gases.

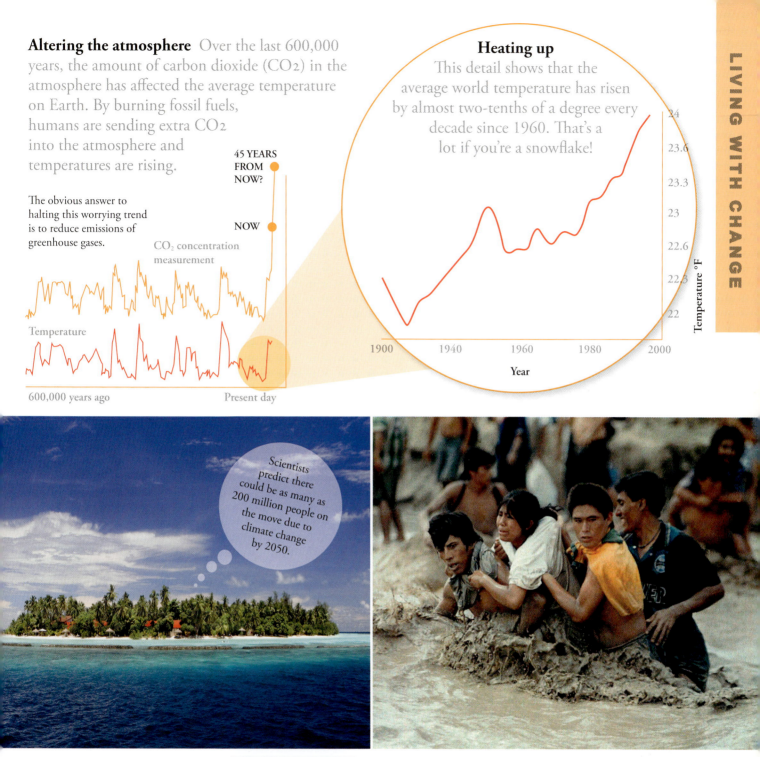

CO_2 concentration measurement

45 YEARS FROM NOW?

NOW

Temperature

600,000 years ago

Present day

Heating up
This detail shows that the average world temperature has risen by almost two-tenths of a degree every decade since 1960. That's a lot if you're a snowflake!

Temperature °F

Year

Scientists predict there could be as many as 200 million people on the move due to climate change by 2050.

Sinking islands The Maldives consists of 1,200 tiny islands peeping out of the ocean. With sea levels predicted to rise by more than 2 ft (.5 m) in the next century, some of the islands could disappear. The Maldivians are preserving the coral reefs that form a natural barrier against tidal surges, and planting trees to prevent beach erosion. Ultimately, they rely on powerful countries to reduce carbon emissions...

Antarctic ice melting affects sea levels worldwide.

Floods With rising sea levels and heavier rain, floods will be more common in many places. A warm current called *El Niño*, which brings heavy rain to western South America every few years, seems to be happening more often and more strongly. Countries at extra risk of flooding need to bolster their defenses, and lay disaster-relief plans. Some may have to prepare for an influx of eco-refugees.

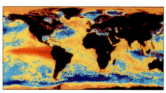

El Niño (in red) moving eastward along the Equator across the Pacific.

243

renewable **energy**

Archeologists of the future will look back at our period of human history and call it the Oil Age—when humans relied on *oil* and other **fossil fuels** for almost everything. The Earth provides many other energy sources, which can be harvested indefinitely and will not run out. With a little ***technology***, we can make fuel or electricity from the wind, the Sun, water, even the Earth itself.

SOLAR ENERGY

Electricity can be generated directly from sunlight, using photovoltaic cells arranged in glass sheets called solar panels. Houses can also use sunlight, instead of a boiler, to heat water by passing it through thin black pipes on a flat surface on the roof. Solar power plants have tens or hundreds of photovoltaic or water-heating solar panels. There is huge potential to generate electricity this way in the world's deserts.

Solar panels at a solar power plant in Rancho Seco in California. In the background is part of a nuclear power plant that is now closed.

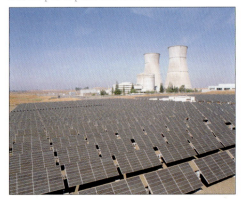

BIOFUELS

Sugary crops like corn are made into bioethanol, which can run gas-powered cars. Oily crops like soybeans or sunflower are made into biodiesel. Food crops aren't the only thing you can use, though. It's possible to make fuel from grass, wood chips, and even wastes such as shredded paper, sawdust, and dung.

Corn

Dung

Hydroelectricity uses the movement of water as it gushes through a dam.

WATER POWER

When you dam a large river, energy builds up behind the dam in a reservoir. Open a gate and water rushes through fast enough to drive a turbine. Worldwide, the amount of energy generated this way has more than doubled since the 1970s.

WIND POWER

A big wind turbine can make two megawatts of power at full speed. That's enough to power more than 1,000 homes. Wind power plants can be built on land or in the sea.

GEOTHERMAL ENERGY

"Geo" means Earth; "thermal" means heat. It is warmer underground, especially in geologically active areas where hot rocks create hot springs. The heat can be used to warm water or generate electricity. In Iceland, most houses are heated geothermally, by piping heat out of the ground. Five percent of California's electricity is generated from underground heat. Even in places without hot springs, it's possible to heat buildings during winter this way, because even when the air gets cold, the ground stays a great deal warmer.

Energy from the Earth

using energy well

Energy-efficient housing Experts say it would be possible to cut world greenhouse gas emissions in half by 2020, just by saving energy and doing things more efficiently. Houses of the future will be less wasteful and make better use of the power of nature.

INSULATION

Insulation, usually fiberglass or wool, goes between the walls and under the floors and roofs. It stops heat from escaping, or getting in, so you use less energy heating or cooling your inside space.

ENERGY EFFICIENT LIGHTBULBS

These fluorescent bulbs use one-fifth of the power that incandescent bulbs use to shine the same light. They last much longer, too.

UNDERFLOOR HEATING

Heat rises, so the most efficient way to heat rooms is from underneath.

REED BED FILTRATION

Dirty water can be cleaned by running it through reed beds in the yard.

MATERIALS

Bricks and concrete take lots of heat energy to make. Building with other materials, such as these recycled shipping containers, is better for the environment.

We can reduce *pollution* by using less energy or energy from renewable sources. Helping the Earth starts at home...

SOLAR PANELS

Solar panels can generate electricity or heat water even when it is cloudy. More than half of all the world's solar electricity is generated in Germany, where overcast weather is more common than sunshine.

PASSIVE SOLAR HEATING

Sunlight streaming through a window heats up the inside space. With careful design, this heat can be gathered in the winter, when the Sun is low in the sky, and avoided in the summer.

Imagine living here...

New technology can help in many ways

Here are some new ideas to save energy, pollute less, or cope in the face of climate change.

WIND-UP RADIO

Electricity can be generated just by turning a handle. Wind-up power can run radios, flashlights, and cell phones.

FLOATING HOUSES

Plenty of towns and cities will flood more with climate change. In the Netherlands people have begun building aluminum houses that float. These houses can be linked by walkways, so whole communities can live on the sea.

DYNAMIC DEMAND

Fridges run all the time. But they can be programmed to turn off temporarily without losing their cooling function when lots of power is being used elsewhere. If all fridges did this, national electricity grids would work more efficiently.

WAVE FARMS

The heave of the ocean waves can be used to make electricity. As seawater fills and empties a chamber, air forced in and out can drive a turbine. Wave energy is not used much yet, but could provide a huge power source.

VIDEO CONFERENCING

Modern telecommunications make it possible for people in different parts of the world to have meetings where all the participants can see and hear each other on screen. This saves a lot of air travel.

RENEWABLE VEHICLES

Cars and buses can run on renewable energy. This bus is powered by hydrogen. As long as the hydrogen is extracted from water using renewable electricity, there is little damage to the environment.

247

MAKING A DIFFERENCE

Better habits at home

use less energy at home

Wash clothes at a lower temperature. Try a lower setting on your washing machine. Your clothes will still come out clean.

Hang your laundry out to dry. Dryers are very energy-hungry so let the wind dry your clothes when it's warm outside.

Reuse your bathwater. You could use dirty bathwater to water houseplants or bathe the dog.

Take showers instead of baths. But keep your shower short, otherwise you may use just as much water and energy.

Don't leave appliances on standby. TVs, phone chargers, and other appliances waste a lot of energy when not in use, so switch them off properly.

Switch off lights when you leave a room. And swap all your bulbs for low-energy ones. Get a wind-up flashlight, too.

Don't overfill kettles or pans. Boiling water takes a lot of energy. Only boil the water you are actually going to use.

Seal the gaps. Use draft protectors under doors and drafty windows. Newspaper, wood, or sealant will also do the job.

Lower your heating by one degree. It won't feel much colder and it will save energy and money.

Adjust your clothing. If you're cold, put on a sweater or vest, rather than turning on a heater. If you're too hot, close the blinds.

shopping for food

Try to buy food with less packaging
You will produce less trash, and, since packaging adds to the cost of your food, you might even end up saving money too.

Buy local and seasonal food Local food doesn't have to travel miles by road or air to reach you. Seasonal food hasn't had to grow in an expensively heated greenhouse. It's probably fresher and healthier, too.

Grow your own! Not only is the food you grow yourself very fresh (you just pick, cook, and eat), but gardening is also good exercise and fun.

Think about it, chew it over

248

Remember to reduce, reuse, and recycle, and you'll save energy, money, and the Earth!

reusing and recycling

Don't throw out old clothes Give them a new lease of life by customizing them or donate them to charity. Those that are too worn can be cut up and used as rags and cloths for cleaning.

Donate old eyeglasses to charity Some charities collect glasses and sort them for reuse by people in the developing world.

If you love shopping Start browsing in second-hand shops. You can find treasure and it's often very cheap, too!

Collect cans and bottles for recycling There's no reason for these to go to a landfill when they can be collected and reused.

Take sneakers for recycling Some companies take sneakers apart and recycle them, making soles into playground floors, for example.

Make birthday cards yourself Use magazines, packaging, and your imagination. It's fun, and guaranteed to look cool.

take it to the next level

Walk or cycle In heavy traffic, trips of less than 1 mile (1.5 km) can be faster on foot or by bike.

Vacation without flying Travel by car, boat, or train and make the trip part of the vacation.

Buy ethical gifts Buy a practical gift (through a charity) like a donkey for someone who needs it.

Say no to plastic bags Carry a reusable bag and you won't need to accept yet another plastic bag.

Write to congress Political change can achieve more than you can on your own, so say what you think!

But what about the rest of the world?

More than a third of the world's population lives in China and India. In both countries, especially in the cities, people are becoming rich: they live in bigger houses, own cars, and use many electrical appliances. But unless they use sustainable forms of energy, this new wealth could have a serious impact on the world's environment.

China is the world's fastest growing economy. It builds a new power plant every week. Most are coal-fired, but the Chinese government also encourages large-scale renewable energy, too.

India has an entire government department dedicated to encouraging renewable energy like solar power and wind power. Like China, it is worried about the rising price of oil, and would rather produce its own energy.

INDEX

Acknowledgments

Dorling Kindersley would like to thank: Iowerth Watkins for cartography; Ed Merritt for additional cartography; Lee Wilson for proofreading; Chris Bernstein for indexing; and Lucy Claxton, Sarah Crowe, Rose Horridge, Emma Shepherd, and Romaine Werblow at the DK Picture Library.

PICTURE CREDITS

The publisher would like to thank the following for their kind permission to reproduce their photographs:
(Key: a-above; b-below/bottom; c-center; f-far; jkt-inside jacket; l-left; r-right; t-top)

4Corners Images: Atlantide Phototravel 189t; Atlantide Phototravel/Stefano Amantino 179clb; **Alamy Images**: 121br; Ace Stock Ltd. 99bc; Peter Adams 103c, 108bl; Aerial Archives 219bl; AfriPics.com 109br; Agripicture Images 122-123; AGStockUSA, Inc. 130cr, 131cr, 135t; Ambient Images Inc 178c (background); Arco Images 43br, 70tl, 92ca, 96c, 167cra, 170-171; Jon Arnold 195br; David Ball 34-35b, 42bl; Robert E. Barber 217fbr; Ricardo Beliel 145bl; Blickwinkel 99bl, 155crb, 156bl, 169l, 197t; Steve Bloom Images 116b; Bobo 32t; Mark Boulton 82-83, 132r, 247tr; G P Bowater 59l; Bryan & Cherry Alexander Photography 46bl, 46br, 47bl, 47br, 52bc; Bruce Coleman Inc 167bc; Andrew Darrington 81tl; Carlos Davila 88br; George S de Blonsky 70r; Danita Delimont 103bc, 175bl; Olivier Digoit 233c; Michael Dwyer 32br, 232r; Eduardo Pucheta Photo 156br; Graham Ella 197bl; Elvele Images 60-61, 195tr; Elvele Images/ CGE 92cb; f1online 124b; Paul Felix Photography 201tl; David Fleetham 230br; John T Fowler 69clb; Clint Garnham 224br; Chris Gomersall 96cra, 97tr; Jane Gould 222cr; David Gowans 174r; Peter Haigh 116c, 118tl, 119ca; Andrew Harrington 118tr; Grady Harrison 135ca; Jennie Hart 28-29cs; Martin Harvey 217tr; Gavin Hellier 98l; Carole Hewer 247cra; Jack Hobhouse 78bl; Andrew Holt 176-177; Holt Studios International Ltd 81tc; Hornbil Images 157bc; imagebroker 180r, 194bc, 194br; Images and Stories 21b, 94t; J L Images 178t; Jacques Jangoux 131bc; Jon Arnold Images / Gavin Hellier 182bl; Peter Jordan 145bc; Juniors Bildarchiv 171tr, 217br; Wolfgang Kaehler 28br; Steven J. Kazlowski 43tr; KLJ Photographic 35clb; Art Kowalsky 179r; Raghunandan Kulkarni/ephotocorp 155tc; Mark Lewis 225br; Lou Linwei 110-111; LOOK Die Bildagentur der Fotografen GmbH 100-101c, 166-167c, jkt; John E

Marriott 179cl; Jenny Matthews 133bl; Philip Mugridge 179bl; NASA Images 13b; David Noble 107t; David Norton 182br; Michael Patrick O'Neill 229bl; Papilio 195bc; Edward Parker 140clb, 144bl, 155l; Photofusion Picture Library 132c; Robert Preston 168l; qaphotos.com 242cl; Seb Rogers 5bl, 162-163, jkt; Galen Rowell/ Mountain Light 57tr; Joern Sackermann 181bl; Robbie Shone 187br; Stephen Frink Collection 204-205; Keren Su / China Span 86-87; tbkmedia.de 201br; Mike Tercek 178b; Dave Thompson 166c; David Tipling 70c; Penny Tweedie 174c, 174l; vario images GmbH & Co KG 135bc; Visual & Written SL 224bl; Visual&Written Sl/Mike Nolan/ VWPics 44crb; David Wall 98br; Lee Warren 194-195c; Dave Watts 189cr; We Shoot 120l; Kim Westerskov 239b; Terry Whittaker 156bc; Wildlife GmbH 37cl, 167bl; Marcus Wilson-Smith 105tr; Worldwide Picture Library 144r, 190r; **Ardea**: Kurt Amsler 226t; Bill Coster 216-217c, 216-217ca; John Daniels 103br; Bob Gibbons 57bc; M. Watson 44br, 61tr, 127r; Andrey Zvoznikov 45bl; **www. atacamaphoto.com**: 95tc, 95tl; Adam Broomberg and Oliver Chanarin: 6tl; **Bryan and Cherry Alexander Photography**: 45fbr, 47bc, 52br, 53br, 53br, 167tr; **Niall Corbet**: 173tl; **Corbis**: 21tl; Peter Adams 102c; Arctic-Images 245b; Yann Arthus-Bertrand 4tr, 90-91, 99t, 188t, 202t, jkt; Atlantide Phototravel 66bl, 84clb, 84-85c; Bjorn Backe/Papilio 101cr; Gary Bell / zefa 239t; Nathan Benn 201c; Niall Benvie 189br; Hal Beral 212ca, 227cra; Tobias Bernhard/zefa 231bc; Andrew Brown 53bl, 143bl; David Butow 107br; Brandon D Cole 222cl; Dean Conger 54-55; Ashley Cooper 214cra; Pablo Corral Vega 175tc; C Devan/zefa 212-213c; EPA 144c, 150bl, 203bl, 242cr, 243cr; ER Productions 88cl; Rig Ergenbright 215bl; Kevin Fleming 71bl, 203t, 205tr; Jose Fuste Raga 215tr, 243cl; Raymond Gehman 101bl, 215br; Walter Geiersperger 175bc, 181t; T Gerson 232l; Farrell Grehan 214cla; Clinch Gryniewicz 218l; H et M/photocuisine 30bl; Tony Hamblin 197bc; Timothy Hearsum 32-33cs; Chris Hellier 159tr; Jeremy Horner 190c; Hulton Archive 214tl; Zen Icknow 237b; JAI / John Coletti 151br; Peter Johnson 53c, 59r; Steve Kaufman 151bl; Kit Kittle 213c; Bob Krist 66t, 71t; T. Kruesselmann / Zefa 247br; Frank Lane Picture Agency 143cr; Jacques Langevin 102br; Frans Lanting 155bc; Frans Lemmens 96br; George D Lepp 17bl; W. Wayne Lockwood, M.D. 84br; Benedict Luxmoore 246-247c; Arthur Morris 51br; NASA 58l; Naturfoto Honal 78br; Baard Ness / Handout/epa 45bc; John Noble 84t, 85ca; Kazuyoshi Nomachi 95br, 98bc; Michael & Patricia Fogden 149br, 151bc; Paul A. Souders 16-17, 125cra; Smiley N. Pool / Dallas Morning News-15733990 191c; James Randklev 186cl; Walter Rawlings / Robert Harding World Imagery 245tr; Jeffrey L Rotman 225bl; Galen Rowell 51bl, 73br; Ron Sanford 50cra, 50tl, 50-51b, 51bc, 51ca, 74-75; Kevin Schafer 215tl; Gregor Schuster 37cl; Joseph Sohm / Visions of America 244-245c; Hans Strand 50ca; Keren Su 104-105c; Sygma 192bl, 192-193c; Roger Tidman 68bl, 230c; Onne van der Wal 214tr; Brian A Vikander 151tl, 151br; Stuart Westmorland 222bc, 232c; Nik Wheeler

200tr; Ralph White 215crb; Witness/Corbis Sygma 57tl; Lawson Wood 227cr; Tim Wright 219br; Xinhua Press 190l; Robert Yin 222br; **DK Images**: Julian Baum 14crb; Malcolm Coulson 88tl; Philip Dowell 112cl; Rose Horridge 89bl; Judith Miller 221tr; Lindsey Stock 248cr; **David Doubilet**: 5tr, 208-209; **Ecoscene**: Paul Ferraby 218c; **Kate Edey**: 225ca; **Mario Farinato**: 181br; **Flickr.com**: cocoleroc 123tr; Linda de Volder 173tr; Mark Eadie 154cr, 203bc; Nathan Eagle 177tr; Manuel Haag 1, 2-3t, 14-15 (background); Jeanie's Pics 119br, Stuart Oikawa 119tl; Luca Patriccioli 203br; Mike Peters 203fbr; Doris Rapp 119fbr; Rodrigo Sala 173cla; Jacob Shamberg 125ca; Jeremy Stone 109bl; Tut99 (Roger) 119bc, Dinesh Valke 155cra; Melanie Yare 195bl; **FLPA**: Jim Brandenburg / Minden 92b; Nigel Cattlin 133t; Tui De Roy/Minden Pictures 56-57c; Danny Ellinger/Foto Natura 103cr; Derek Hall 121bl; David Hosking 120c; S Jonasson 225tc; Francoise Merlet 66b, 85cla, 85cr; Mark Moffett / Minden 73bc; Mark Newman 118cl, 118-119c, 119c; Flip Nicklin/Minden Pictures 56br; Terry Whittaker 183bl; Konrad Wothe 97c; **Getty Images**: Pete Atkinson 221b; W Banagan 37tr; Ira Block 106-107c; Larry Broder 48-49; China Photos 109bc; Ed Darack 71br; Peter David 212bl; Reinhard Dirscherl 227br; Georgette Douwma 223cl, 223cr; Michael Dunning 218r; Bob Elsdale 5c, 184-185, jkt; First Flight 214crb; Raymond Gehman 78-79c; Guillermo Gonzalez 73bl; Ken Graham 52bl; Darrell Gulin 72br; Jeff Harbers/Science Faction 62; Hulton Archive 165bl; Arnulf Husmo 214br; The Image Bank/Joseph Van Os 4bl, 40-41; Chris Johns 217bl; Johnny Johnson 50cb; Tim Laman 5tl, 138-139, 226br, jkt; Frans Lemmens 148-149c; Roine Magnusson 198-199; Ray Massey 213br; Joe McDonald 149bc; Eric Meola 189bl; Kevin Miller 228bl; Minden Pictures/Gerry Ellis 143br; Minden Pictures/Norbert Wu 57fbr; Darlyne A Murawski 213fbl; Paul Nicklen 75tl; Rei Ohara 227fbr; Oxford Scientific Films / Photolibrary 158-159; Pete Oxford 149cr; Andrew Parkinson 154bl; Michael & Patricia Fogden 140bl, 148cl, 148t, 152-153, 153tr, 154bc; Terje Rakke 245tc; Robert Harding World Imagery / James Hager 51fbr; Andy Rouse 148br; Kelly Ryerson 214bl; David Sanger 214clb; Joel Sartore 138cb; Mike Severns 227bl; Anup Shah 146-147; Peter Sherrard 150bc; Marco Simoni 29bl; Brian J. Skerry 212cb, 227fbl; Moritz Steiger 96-97c; Maria Stenzel 62bl, 143bc; Tom Stoddart 157t; Nobuaki Sumida 4c, 64-65; Superstudio 79bl; Darryl Torckler 228bc; James Warwick 65l; Art Wolfe 227bc; Konrad Wothe 50cb, 68-69c; **Clare Harris**: 66ca, 76-77t; **Image Quest 3-D**: 231fbl; **The Irish Image Collection**: Tim Hannan 213bl; **Johns Hopkins University Applied Physics Laboratory/Southwest Research Institute**: 1997 by the Ocean Remote Sensing Group 231tl; **Lonely Planet Images**: Mark Webster 229bc; **Thomas Marent**: 142bl; **Mike Markey**: Mike Markey 225cla; **Walter Muma**: 69br; **NASA**: Johnson Space Center 24b; Goddard Space Flight Center Scientific Visualization Studio 109t; GRIN 14-15c, 23tl, 27t; GSFC / Reto Stoeckli, Nazmi El Saleous &

Marit Jentoft-Nilsen 2-3b; LANDSAT/ University of Maryland Global Land Cover Facility 197t; **naturepl.com**: Karl Ammann 127c; Peter Blackwell 129tr; Cindy Buxton 57bl; Bruce Davidson 149bl; Sue Flood 57br; Graham Hatherley 97bc; Tony Heald 125bl; Dietmar Hill 125fbr; Paul Hobson 173br; Rhonda Klevansky 172-173c; Neil Lucas 125bl; Pete Oxford 149fbr; Peter Oxford 172cl, 172tr; Staffan Widstrand 44-45c; **NOAA**: David Burdick 229ftl, 229tl, 229tr; George E Marshall Album 121t; Dr Dwayne Meadowsreef 229tc; OAR/National Undersea Research Program (NURP) 222tr; **OSF**: Paul Franklin 167br; Rodger Jackman 222fbl; Satoshi Kuribayashi 199tr; Mary Plage 161c; Tui De Roy 45br, 189clb; Survival Anglia 157bl; **PA Photos**: AP Photo 108c, 207br; **Pelamis Wave Power Ltd**: 238bl; Pelamis Wave Power 247cb; **Photolibrary**: ER Degginger 154cl, 155tr; **Photoshot/NHPA**: A.N.T. Photo Library 169c; Pete Atkinson 233r; Nigel J Dennis 125bc; Martin Harvey 124cl, 125c; Adrian Hepworth 150br; Daniel Heulin 97bl; T Kitchin and V Hurst 69bc; Yves Lanceau 102cl; Haroldo Palo Jr 56ca; Andy Rouse 168r; John Shaw 49tr; Mirko Stelzner 103fbr; **Pro Natura Zentrum Aletsch**: Laudo Albrecht 181bc; **PunchStock**: Digital Vision 220; Photographer's Choice 66cb, 72c (background), 73c (b/g); Stockbyte/ Tom Brakefield 68br; **SaharaMet**: R. Pelisson 17r; **Science Photo Library**: Michael Abbey 16bl; NASA 25bl; Mike Agliolo 242t; Steve Allen 243bl; Nick Bergkessel 79bc; Martin Bond 133bc, 244bl, 244br, 247fbl; Dr John Brackenbury 76clb; Massimo Brega 135cb; British Antarctic Survey 59c; Robert Brook 35cr; Tony Craddock 240-241, 242bl; Christian Darkin 12cl; Georgette Douwma 85br; Michael Dunning 18cl; European Space Agency 14ca; P G Adam, Publiphoto Diffusion 39; Bob Gibbons 200b; Andy Harmer 198bc, 198bl, 198br; Jan Hinsch 233l; Manfred Kage 58c; LEPUS 213bc; Dr Ken Macdonald 17bc; NASA/ESA/Stsci/R, schaller 4tl, 10-11; NASA/Goddard Space Flight Center Scientific Visualization Studio 58r; NOAA 210bl, 242br, 243br; Merlin D Tuttle 101tc; Detlev van Ravenswaay 13c, 15t, 24t; M I Walker 19cl; Jason Ware 12t; **Michael Scott**: 155br, 157br, 161t, 179cla; **SeaPics.com**: 229ftr; Clay Bryce 228br; Bob Cranston 231br; Steve Drogin 235tl; Richard Herrmann 234-235, jkt; Espen Rekdal 222bl, 231bl, jkt; Dennis Sabo 223bl; Mark Strickland 234clb; Ron and Valerie Taylor 235tc; Masa Ushioda 227cl, 229br, 235tr; Marli Wakeling 226bl; James D Watt 226c; **Mark W Skinner @ USDA-NRCS PLANTS Database**: 169r; **stevebloom.com**: 231c; Steve Bloom 4br, 114-115, 128-129, jkt; **Still Pictures**: Gil Moti 113bc; Jorgen Schytte 196r; Silke Wedler 112-113bc; **Sublette County Historical Society**: 193tr; **SuperStock**: age fotostock 8, 97br; **TrekEarth**: Tsetsegee Sumiya 103bl; **UNEP**: 106b; **US Geological Survey**: 229cl; **USDA Forest Service (www.forestryimages.org)**: Darren Blackford 70bl; **www.UWPhoto.no**: Erling Svenson 225bc

All other images © Dorling Kindersley
For further information see:
www.dkimages.com